Adult Coloring Book Series

The Magic Mandala Coloring Book

50 Mandala Designs For Stress Relief, Relaxation and
Art Therapy (Volume 2)

Michelle Shea

A Note From The Author

Thank you for purchasing The Magic Mandala Coloring Book.

Beginning at the next page you will find 50 mandala illustrations for your coloring pleasure. The 50 mandalas in this volume is a mix of simple and more intricate drawings to suit a range of preferences.

This book is part of the Adult Coloring Book Series-Mandalas. If you enjoy this book, please take a look at the other coloring titles at the back cover of this book. You will certainly find plenty of outstanding coloring pages to keep you active and entertained.

You will notice that there is just one design per page and the back is left blank. This is done on purpose so that should the colors bleed through to the back page, they do not ruin the mandalas.

You may wish to put a thin sheet of cardboard between pages to prevent the ink from bleeding through to the following pages when using gel pens or markers to do your coloring. Or you could choose coloring utensils like pencils that will not bleed through the paper. Do be aware however that if you press a hard tipped surface to the page, such as when using a ball-point pen, it may leave a depression on the page behind your current coloring surface.

With these thoughts in mind, I urge you to get ready your pencils, crayons, markers or whatever you prefer to color or paint in and have a great time coloring the pages in this book.

Before I leave, I have a quick favor to ask and will appreciate if you please take **one minute** to leave a **personal review** of this book on the sales page. It is a fact that my future success as a coloring book author is directly tied to the number of people talking about my books and it is my sincerest hope that you will find my books worthy of your recommendations. Do also take some time to **post pictures of your colored mandalas** on the Amazon review page for us to ogle and admire!

If you have any questions or fancy a chat, do drop me an email at michelle@amzndownload.com

Enjoy coloring.

Sincerely yours,
Michelle Shea

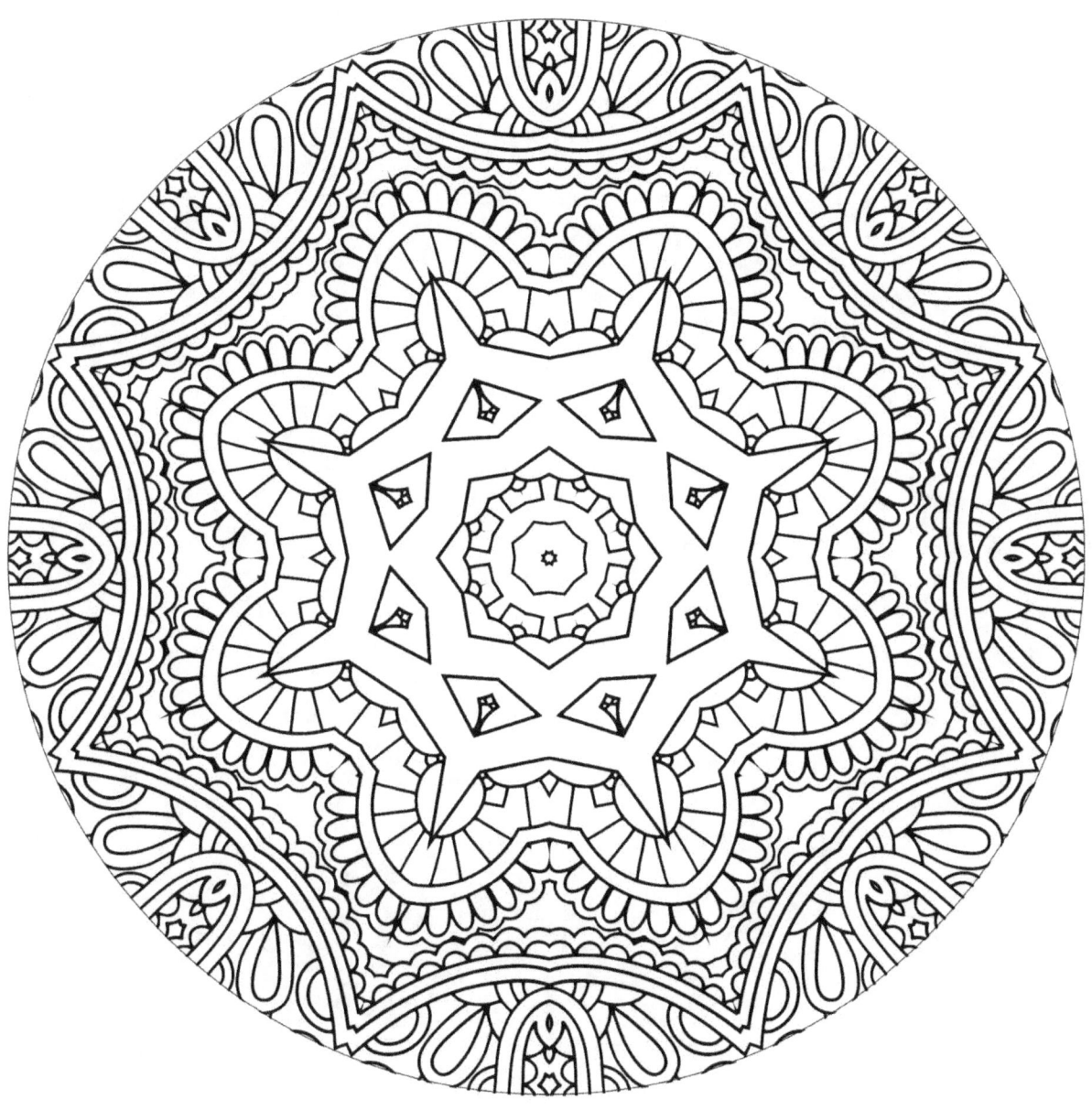

MG1

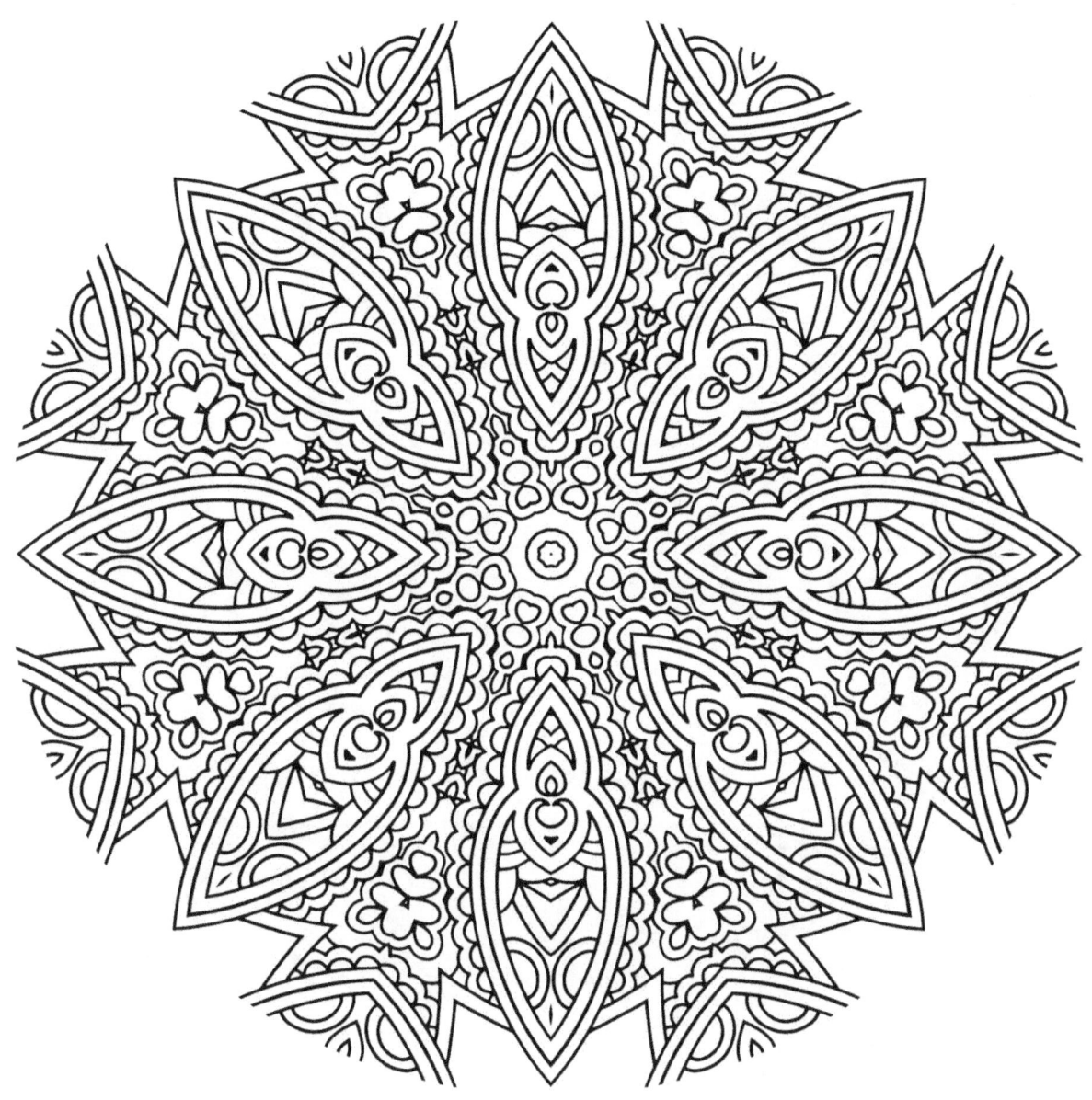

MG2

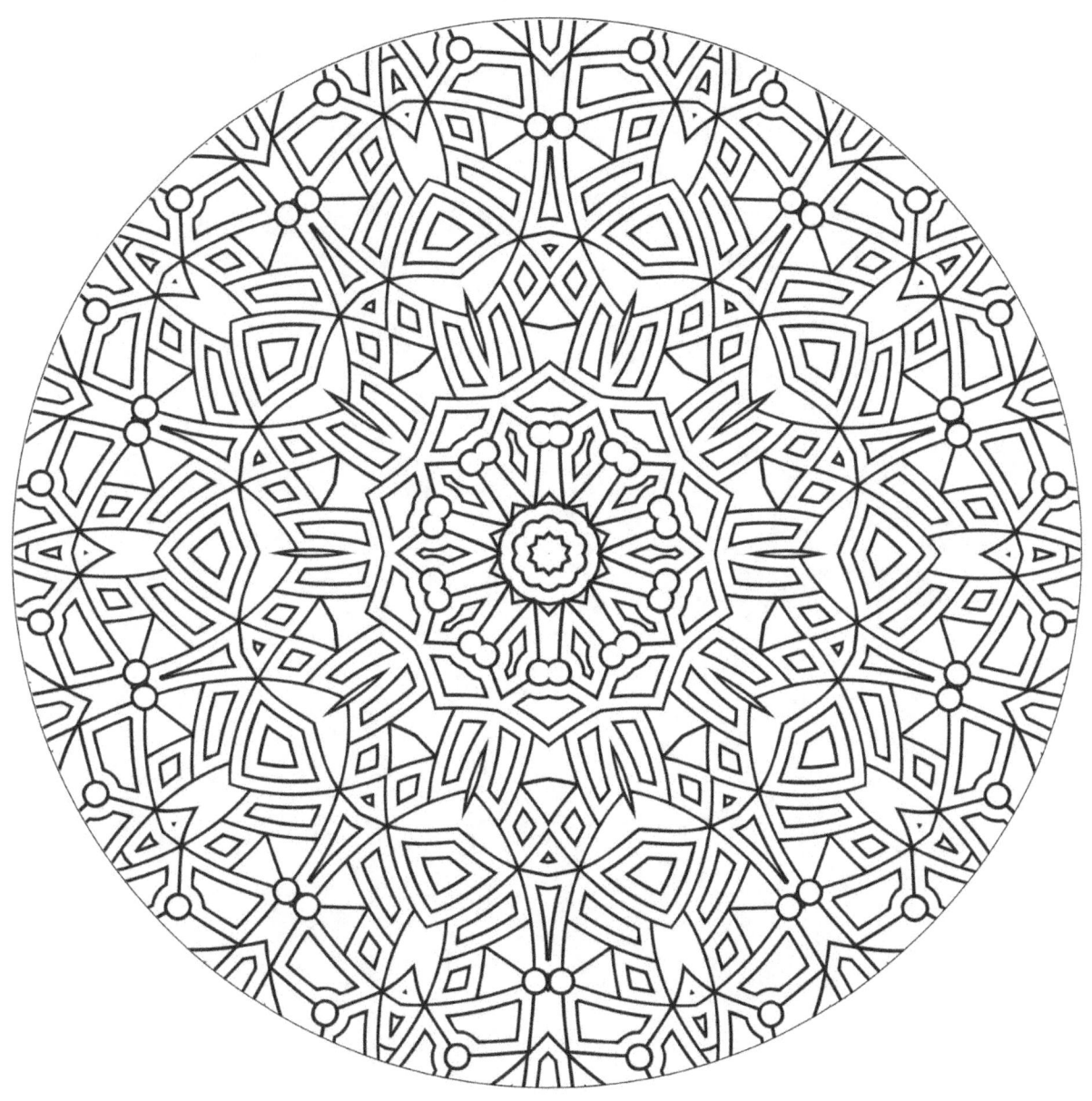

MG3

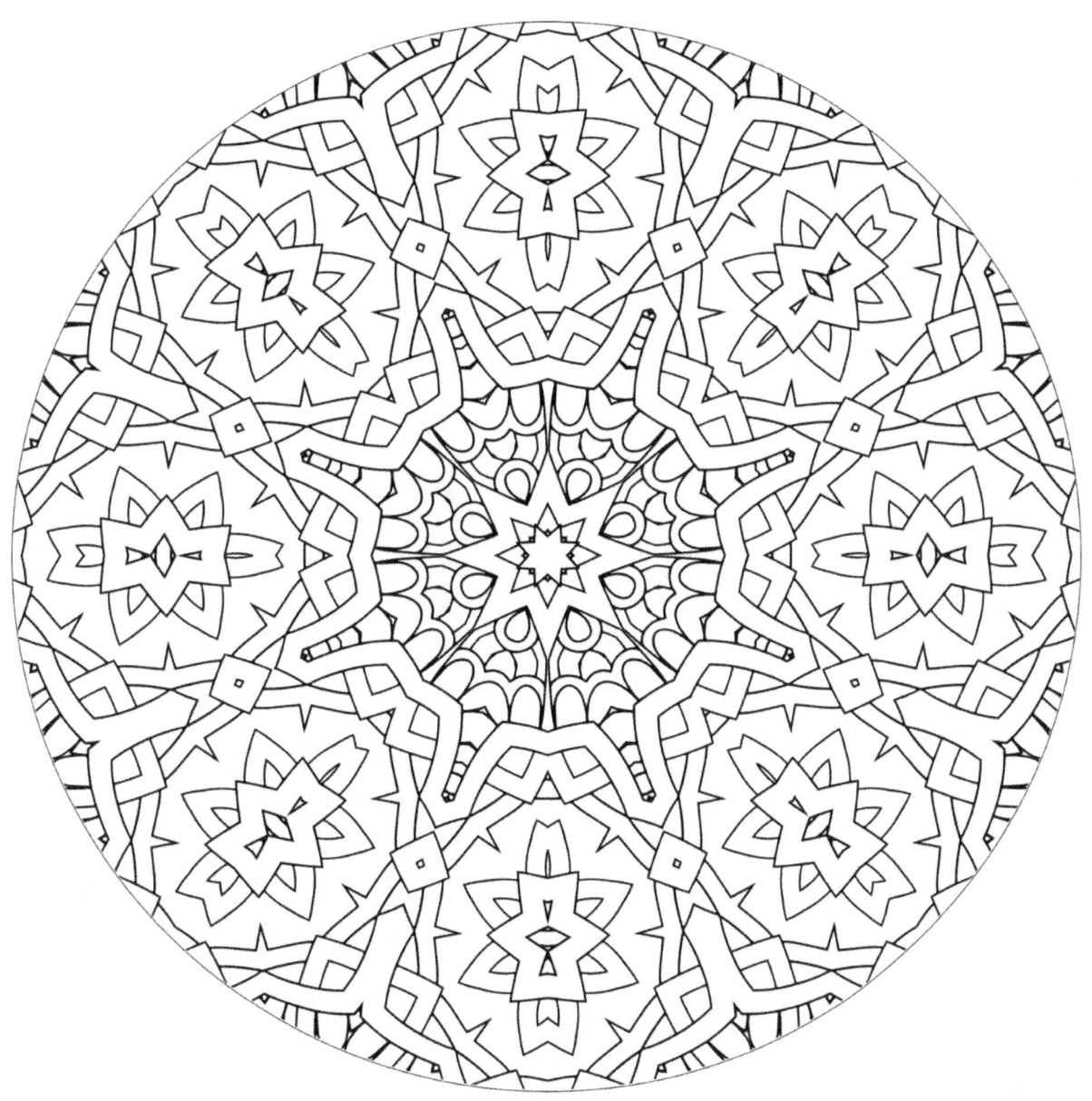

MG4

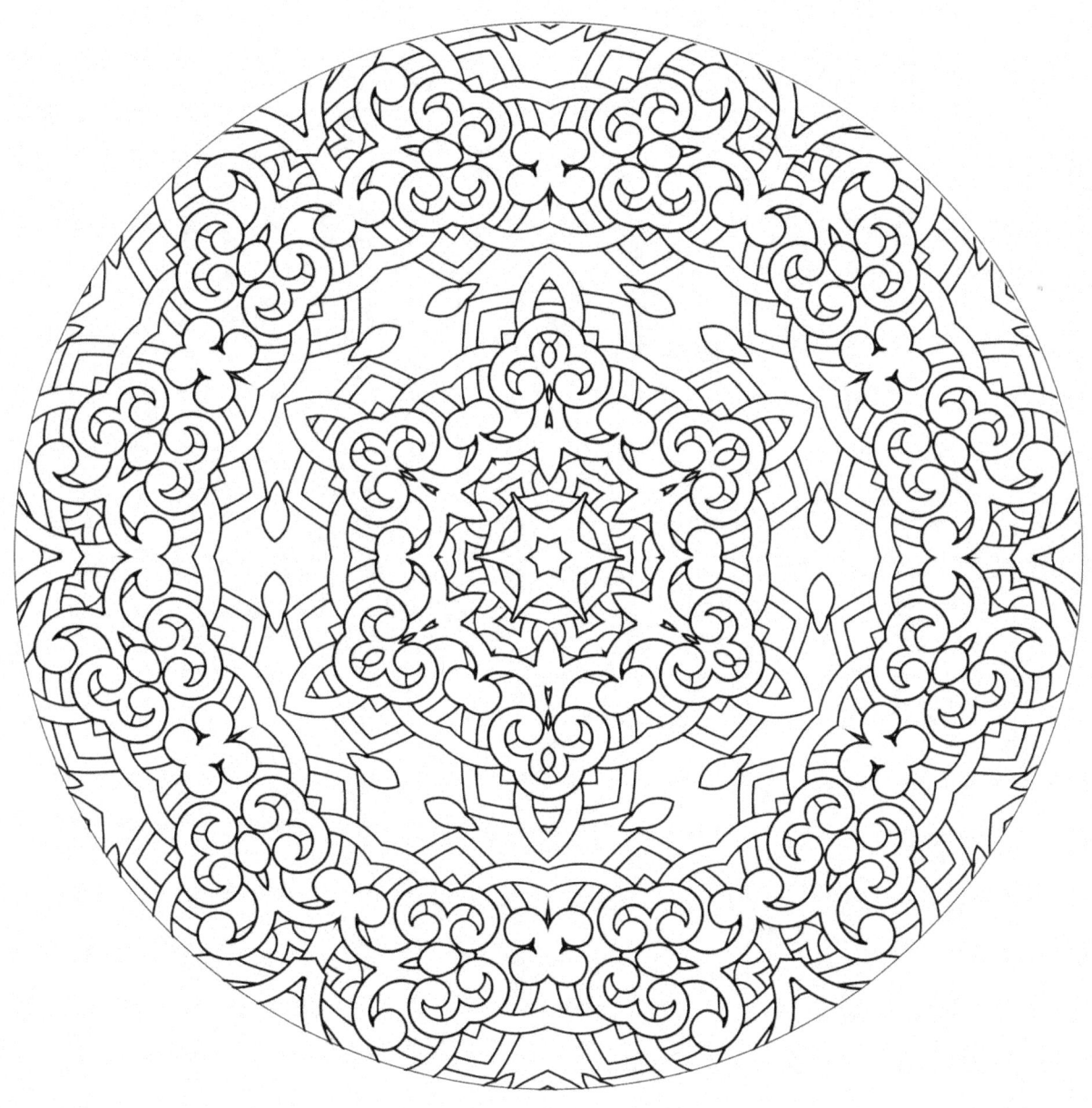

MG5

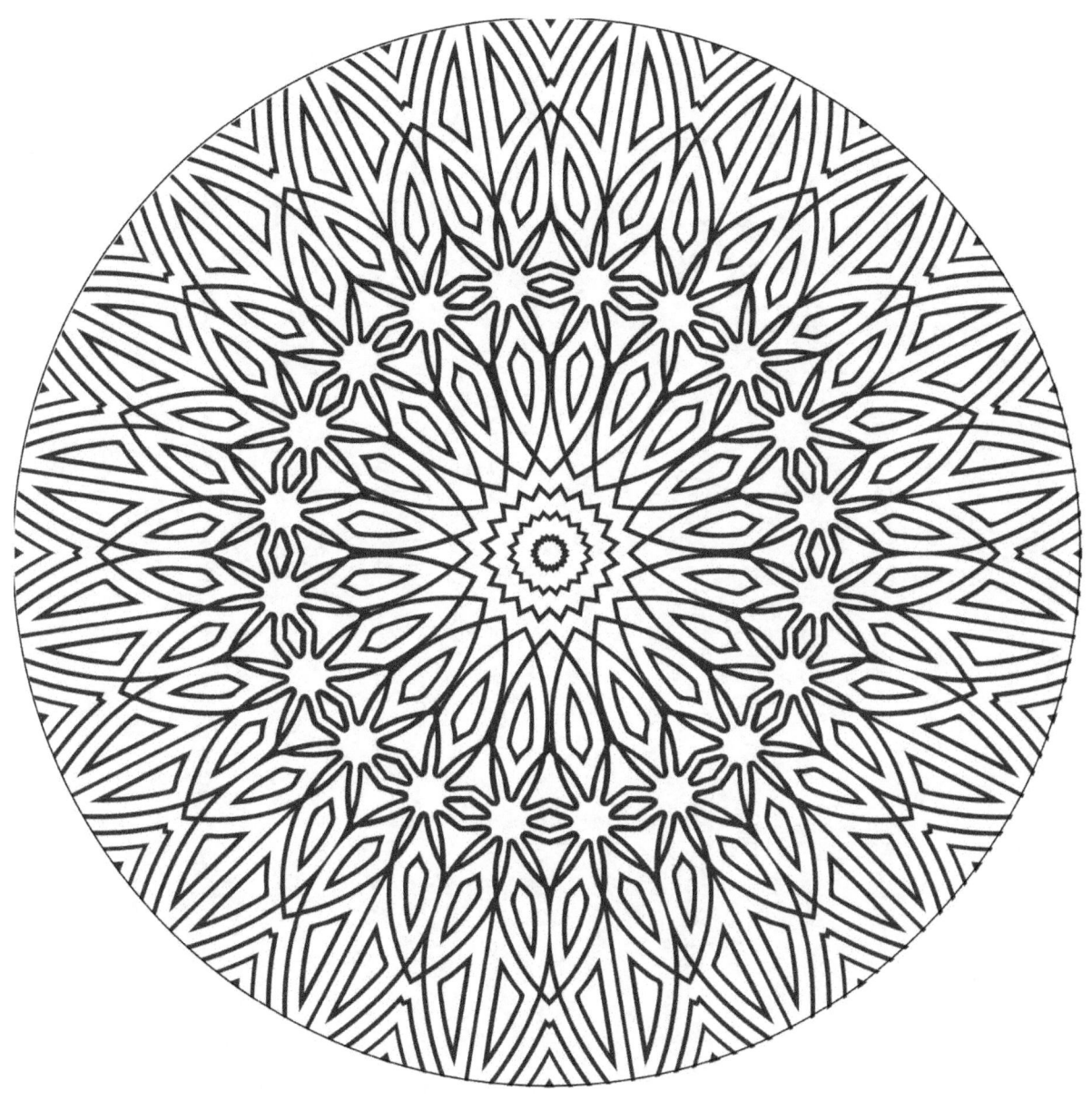

MG6

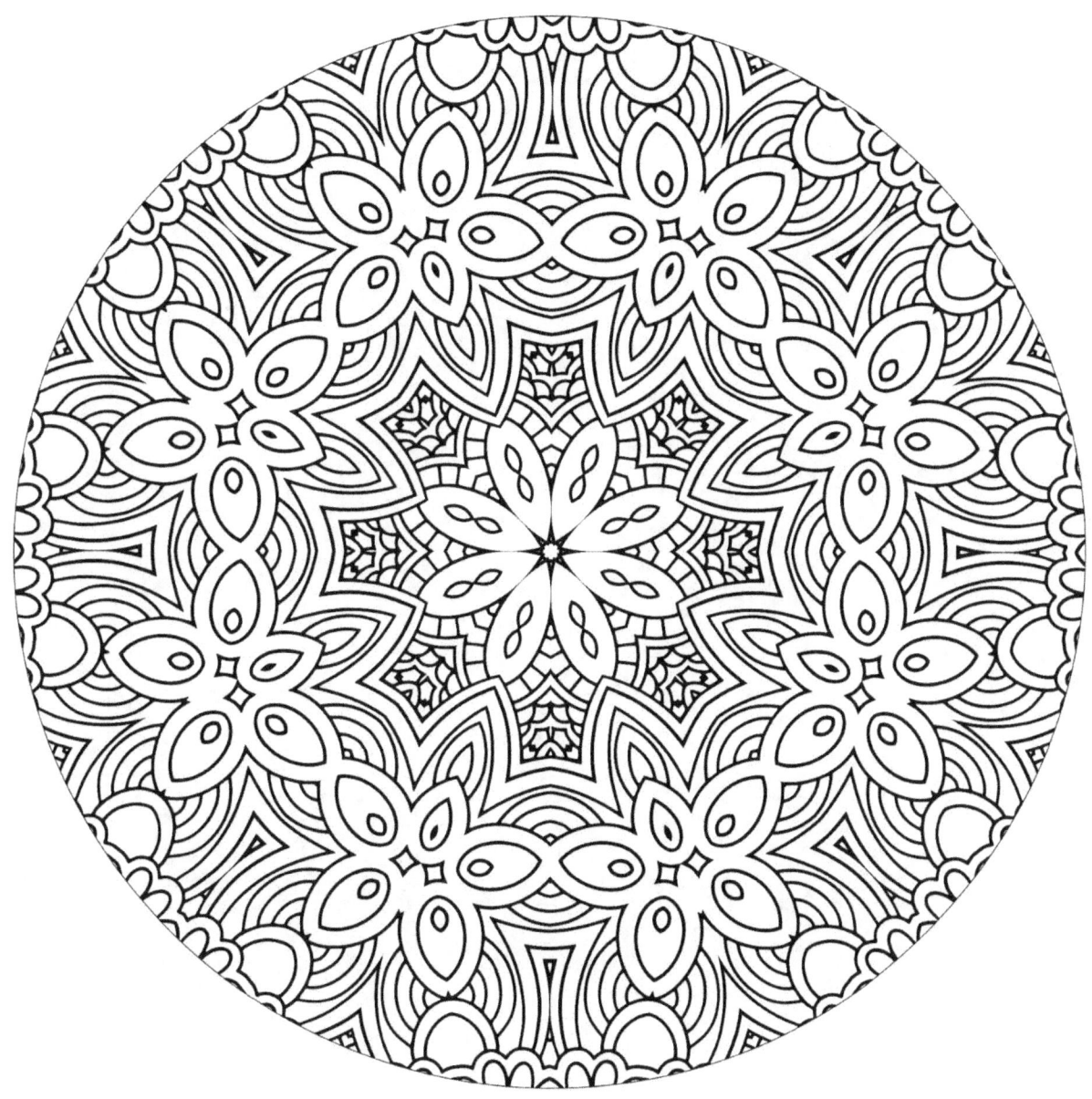

MG7

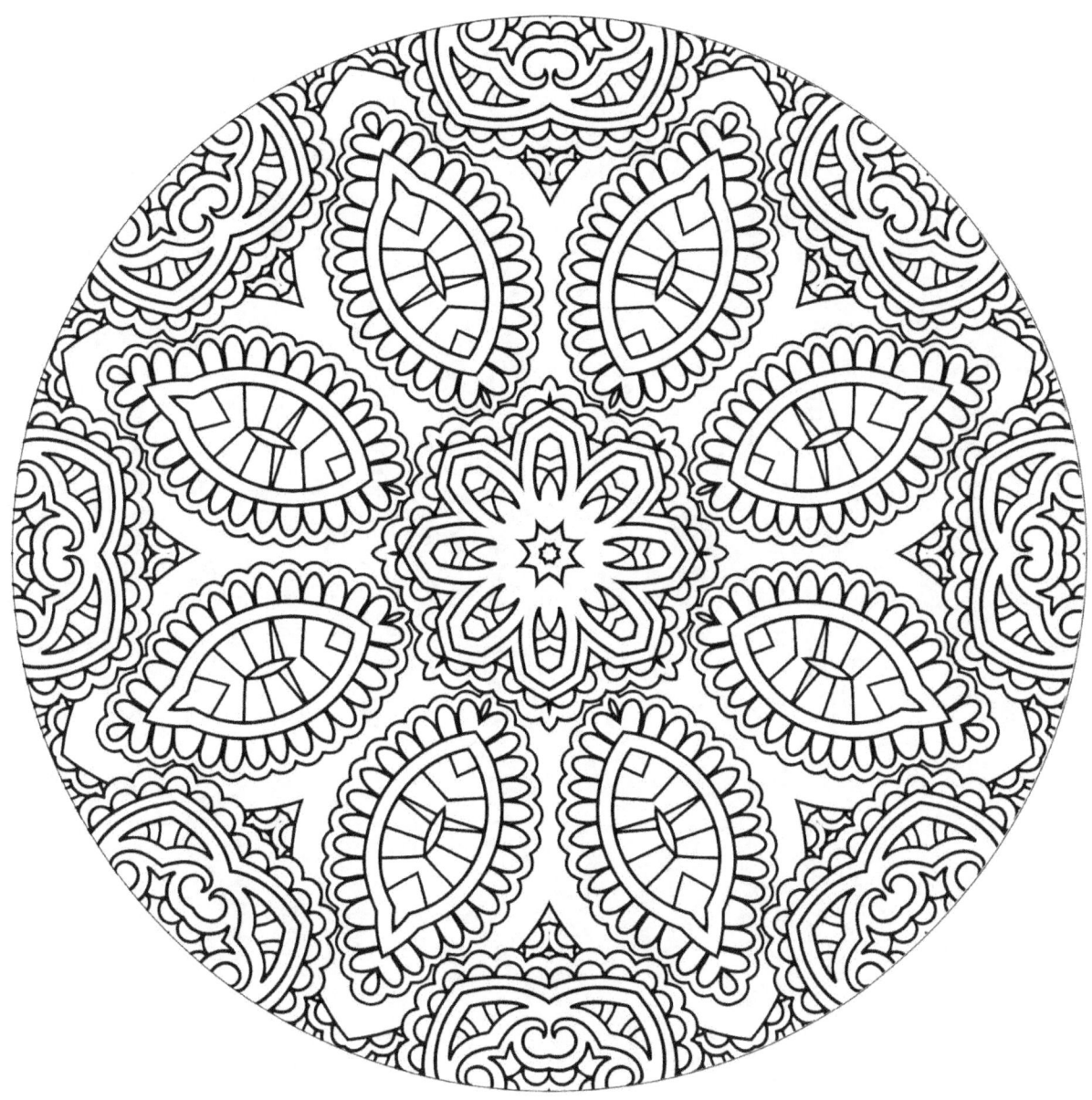

MG8

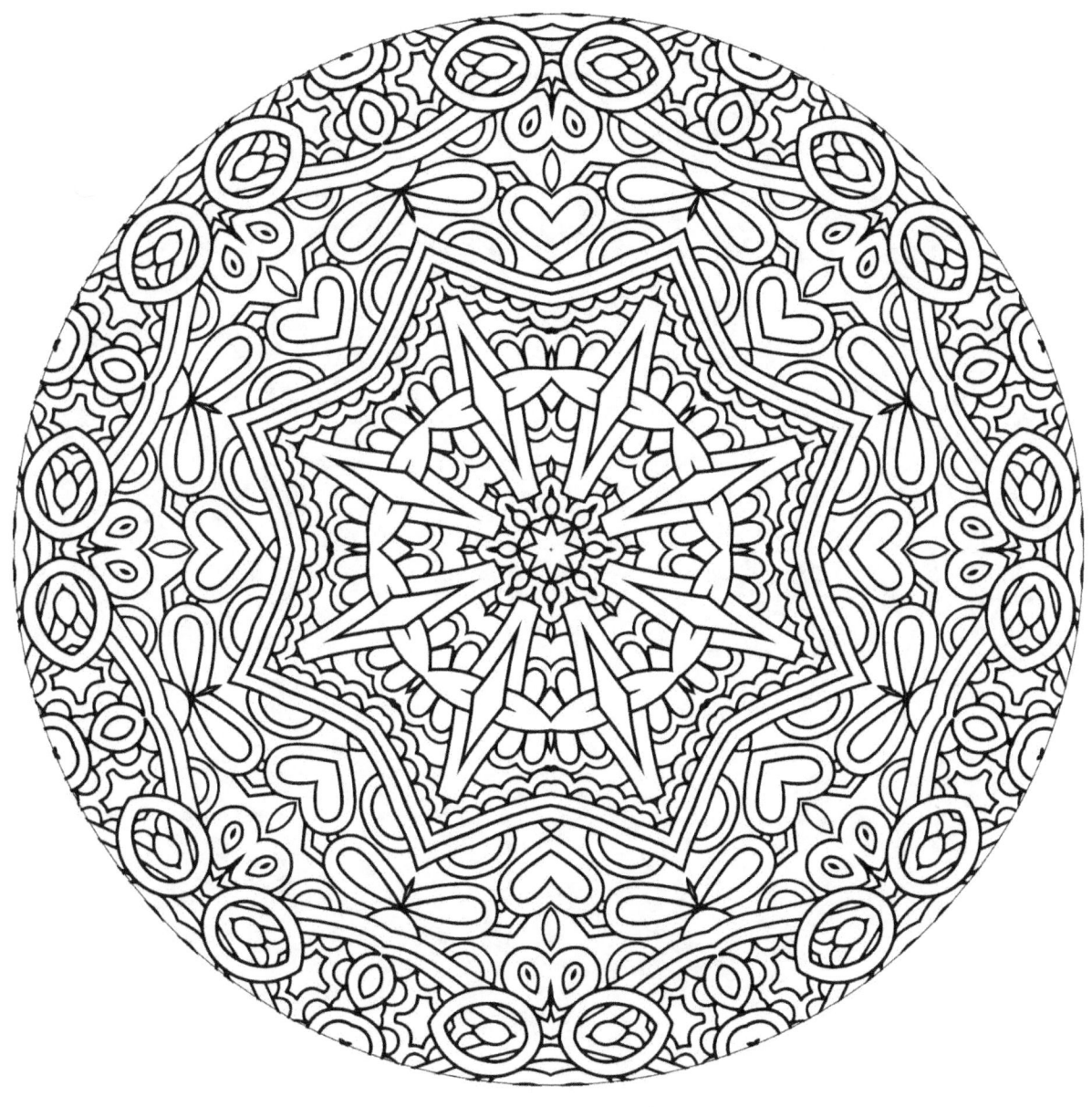

MG9

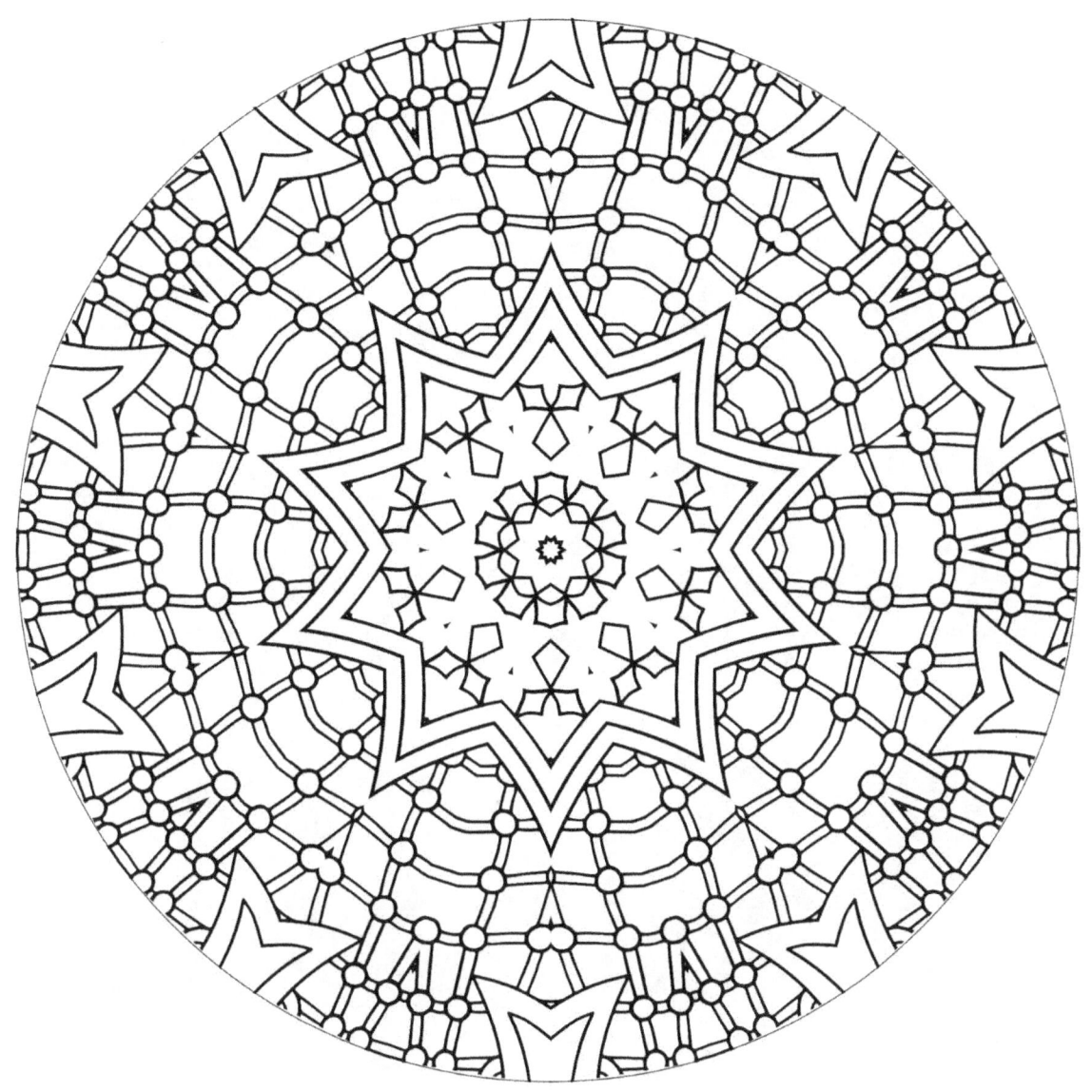

MG10

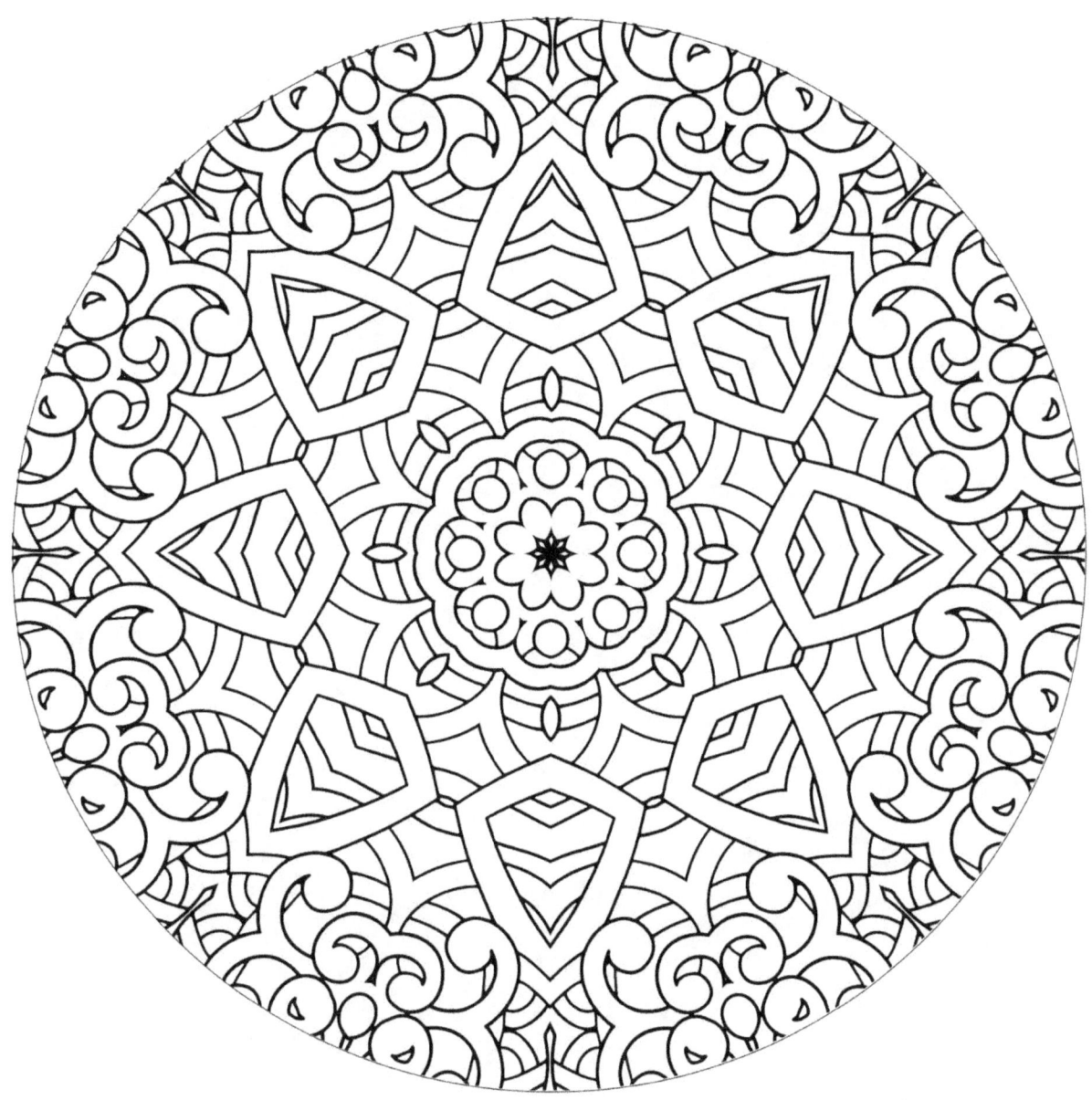

MG11

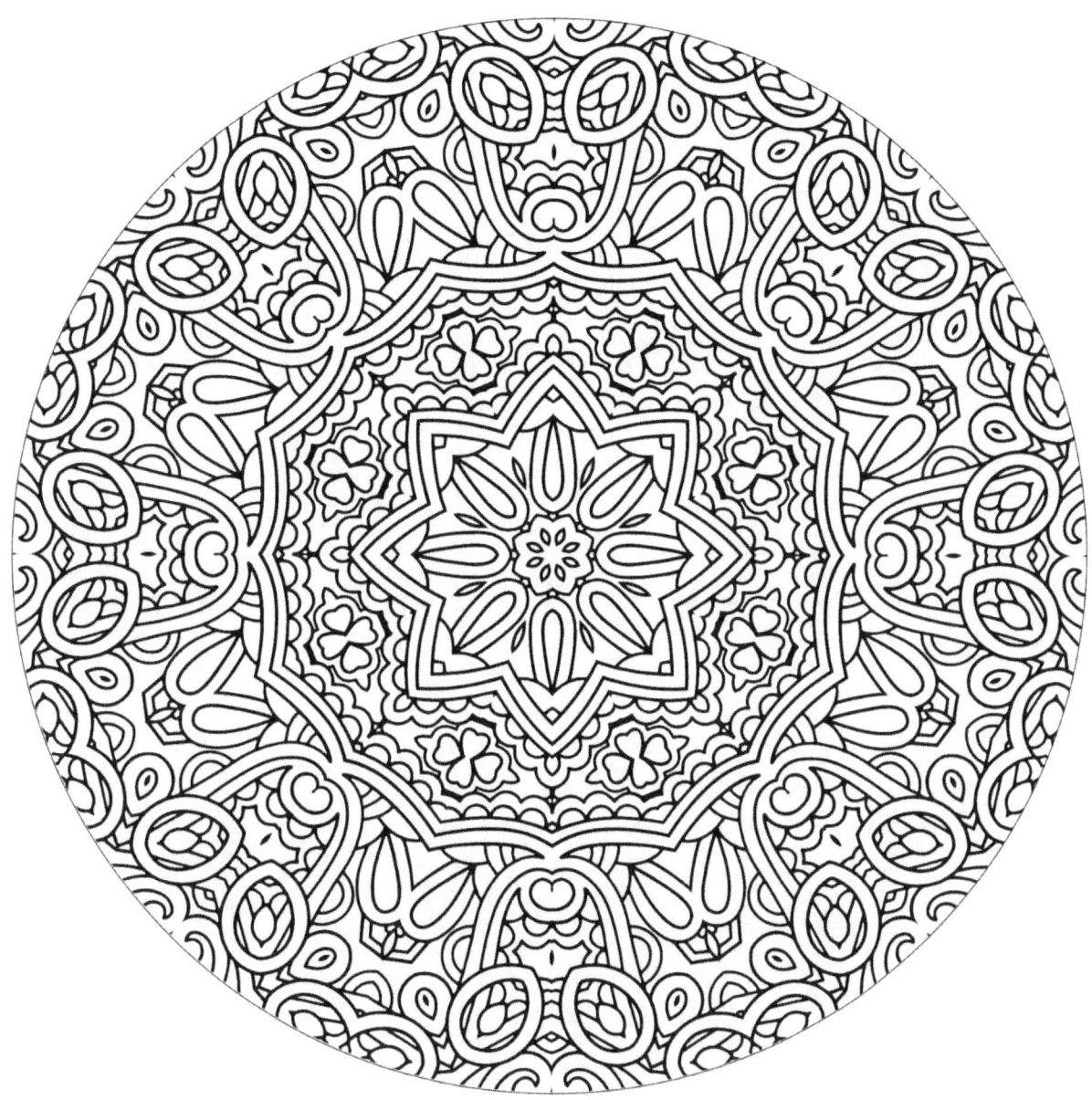

MG12

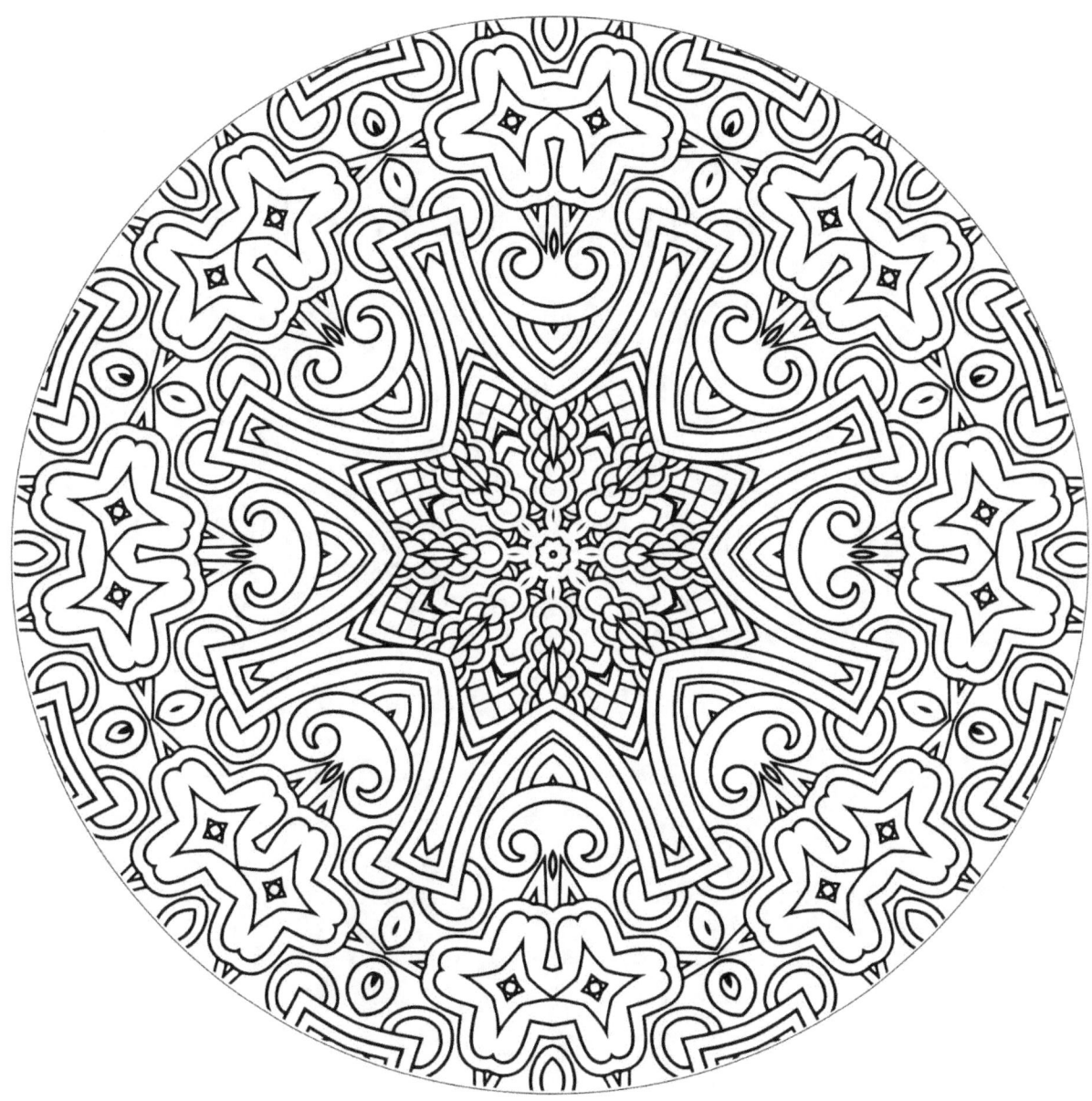

MG13

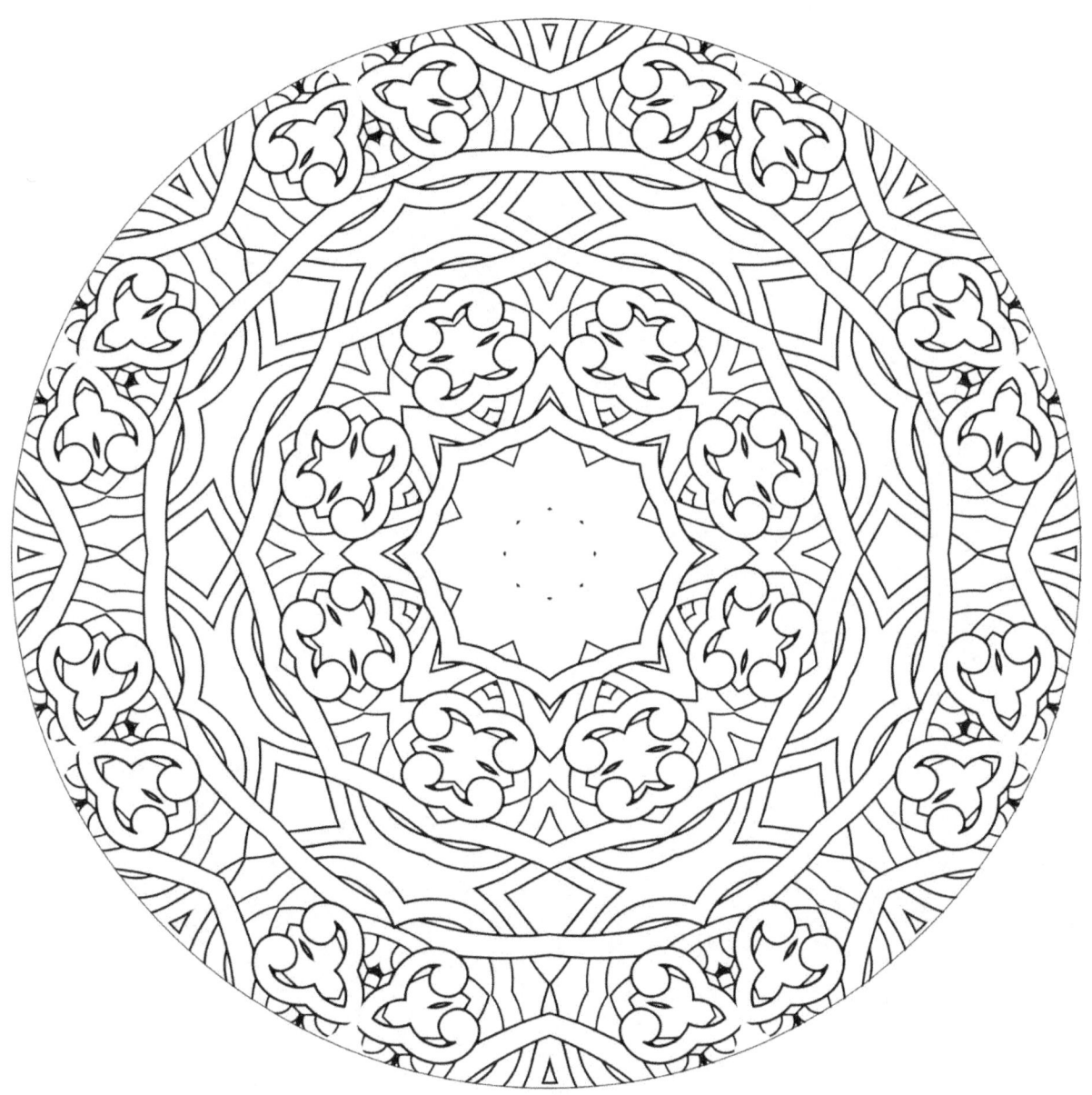

MG14

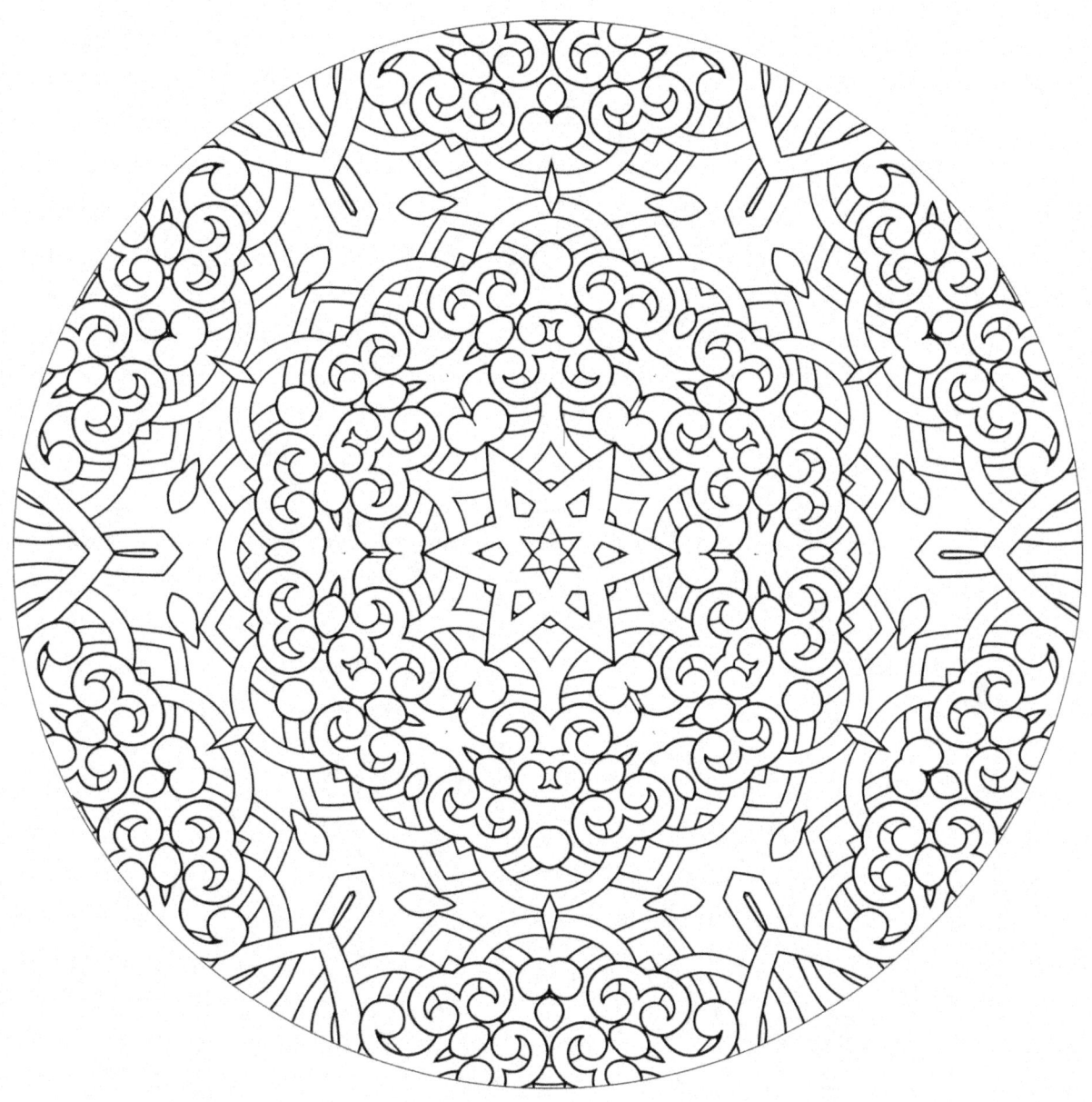

MG15

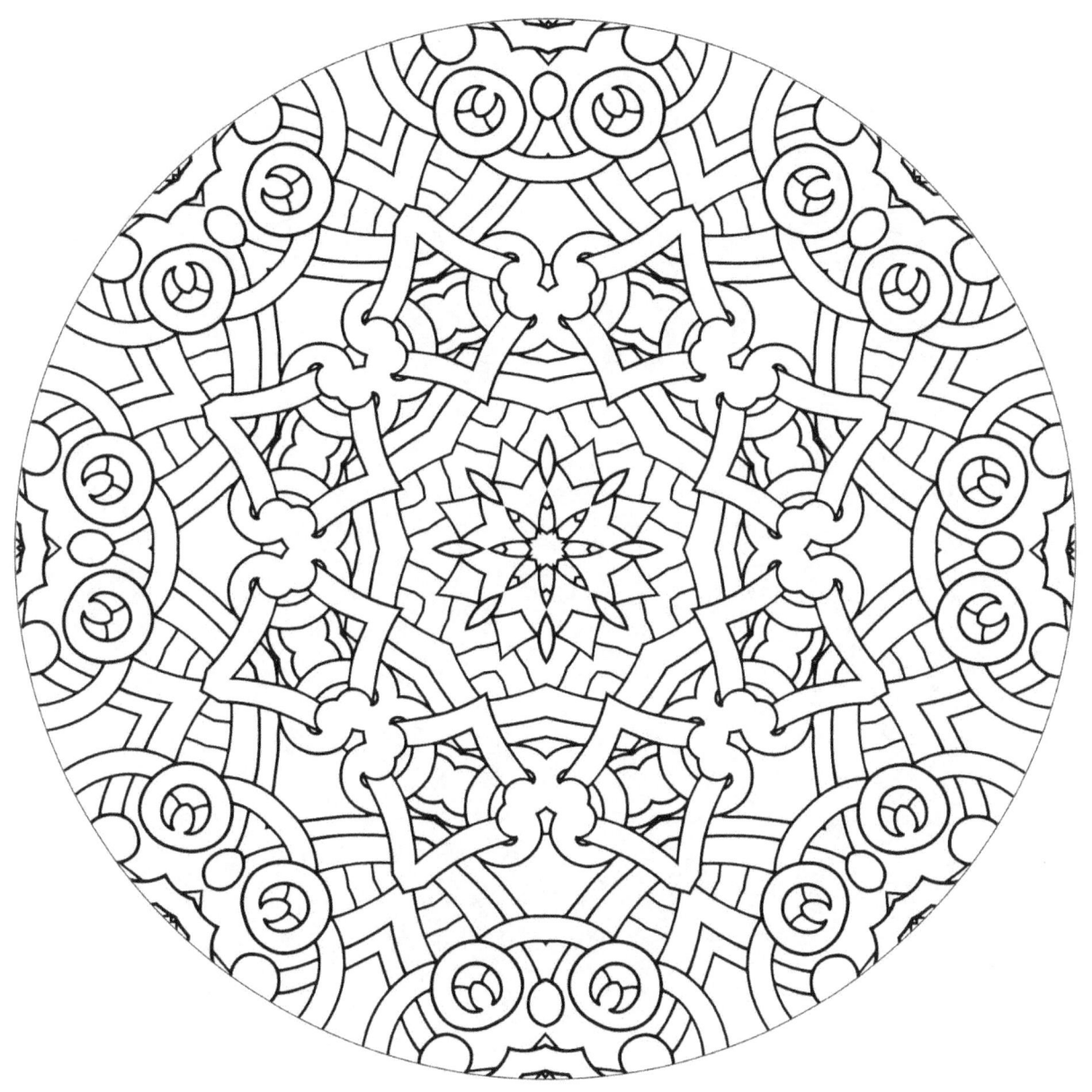

MG16

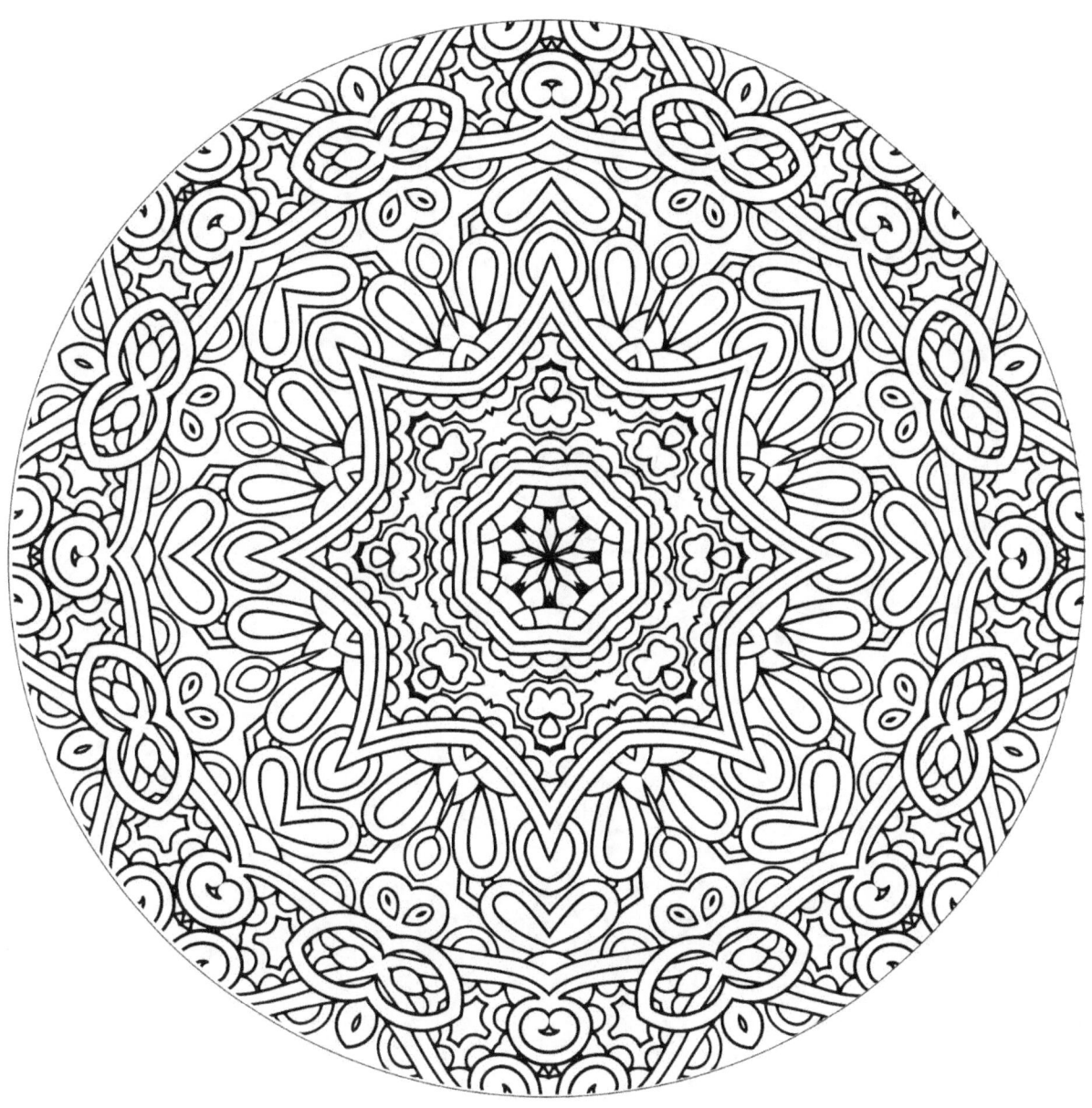

MG17

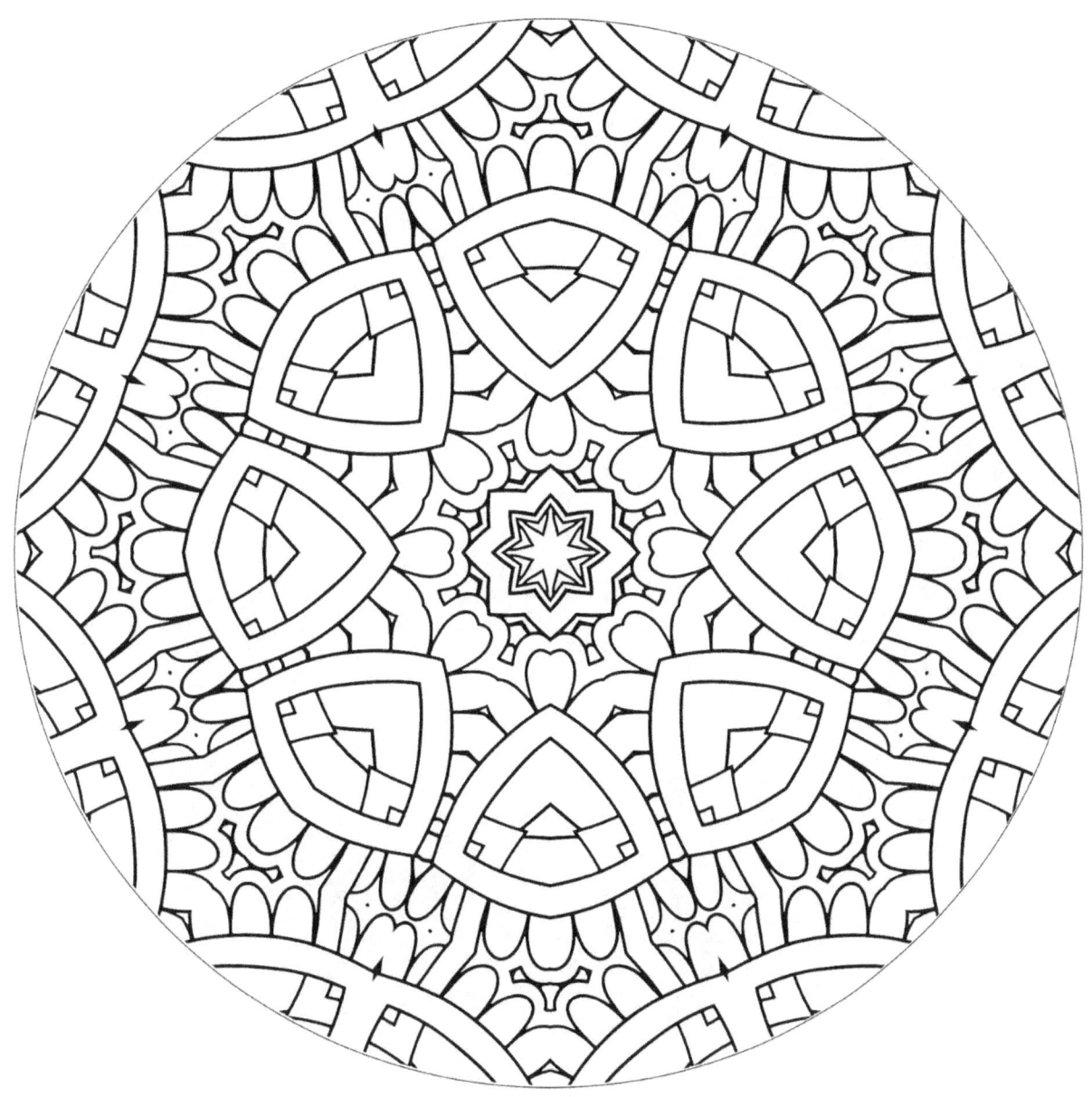

MG18

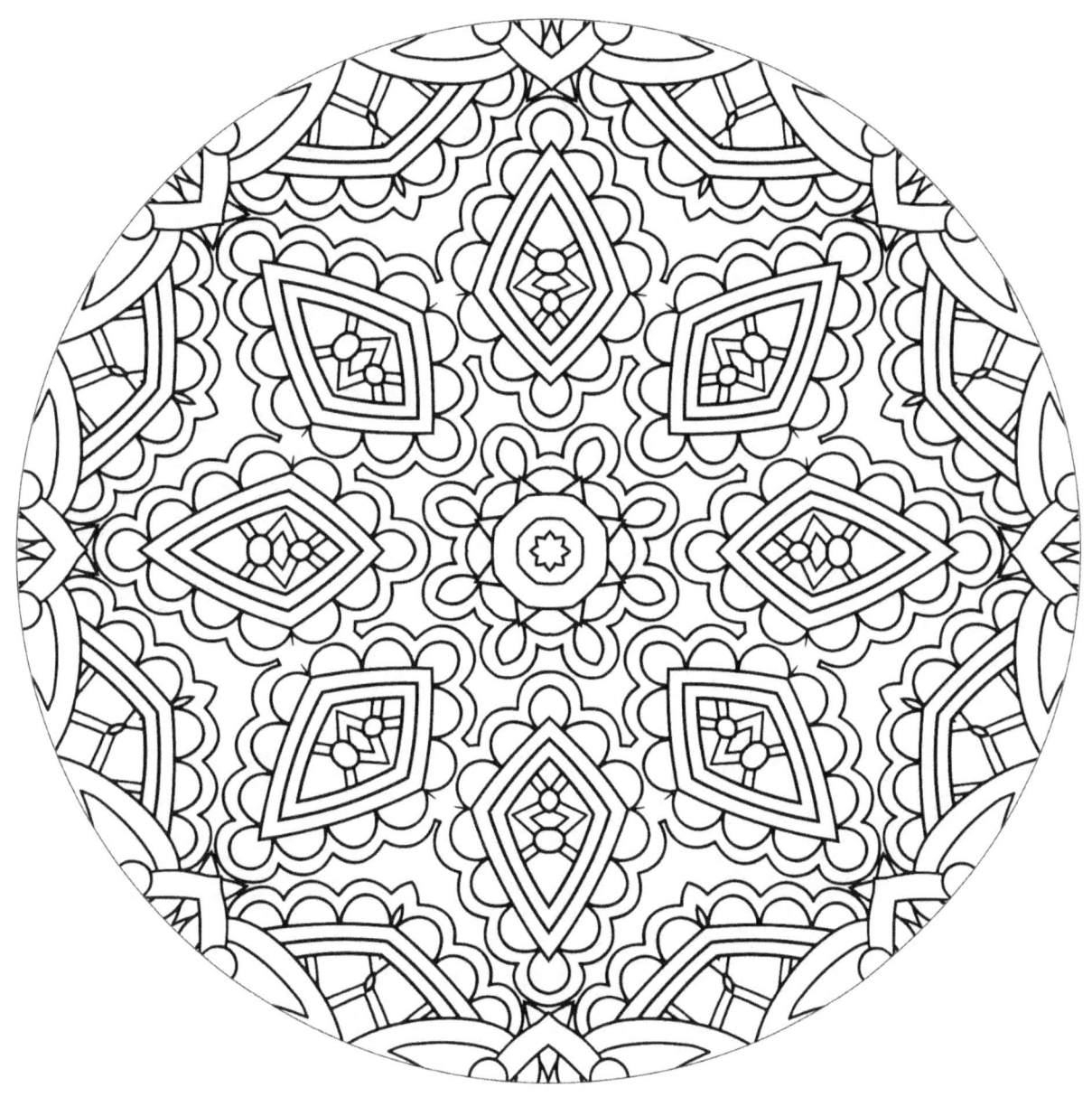

MG19

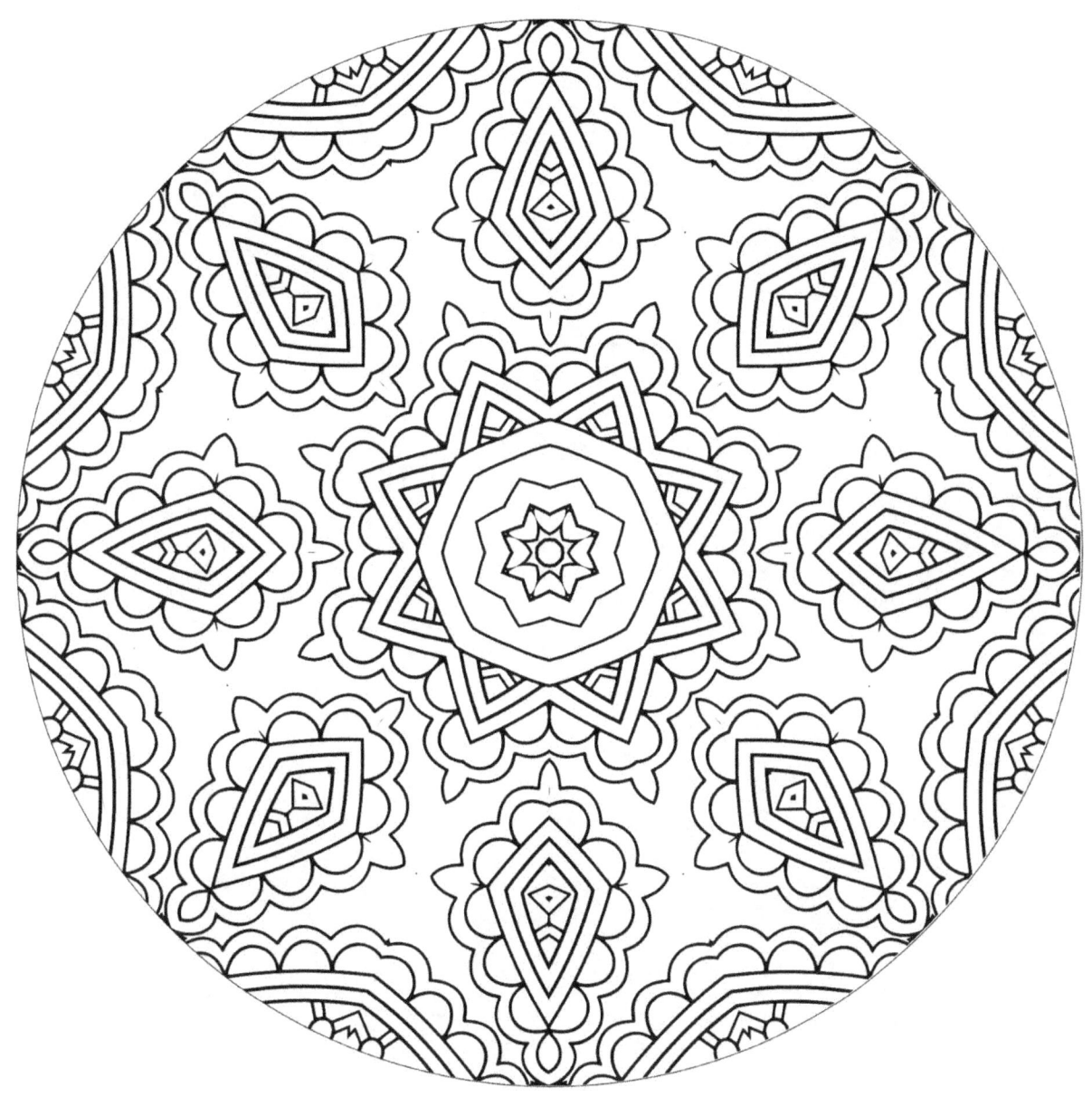

MG20

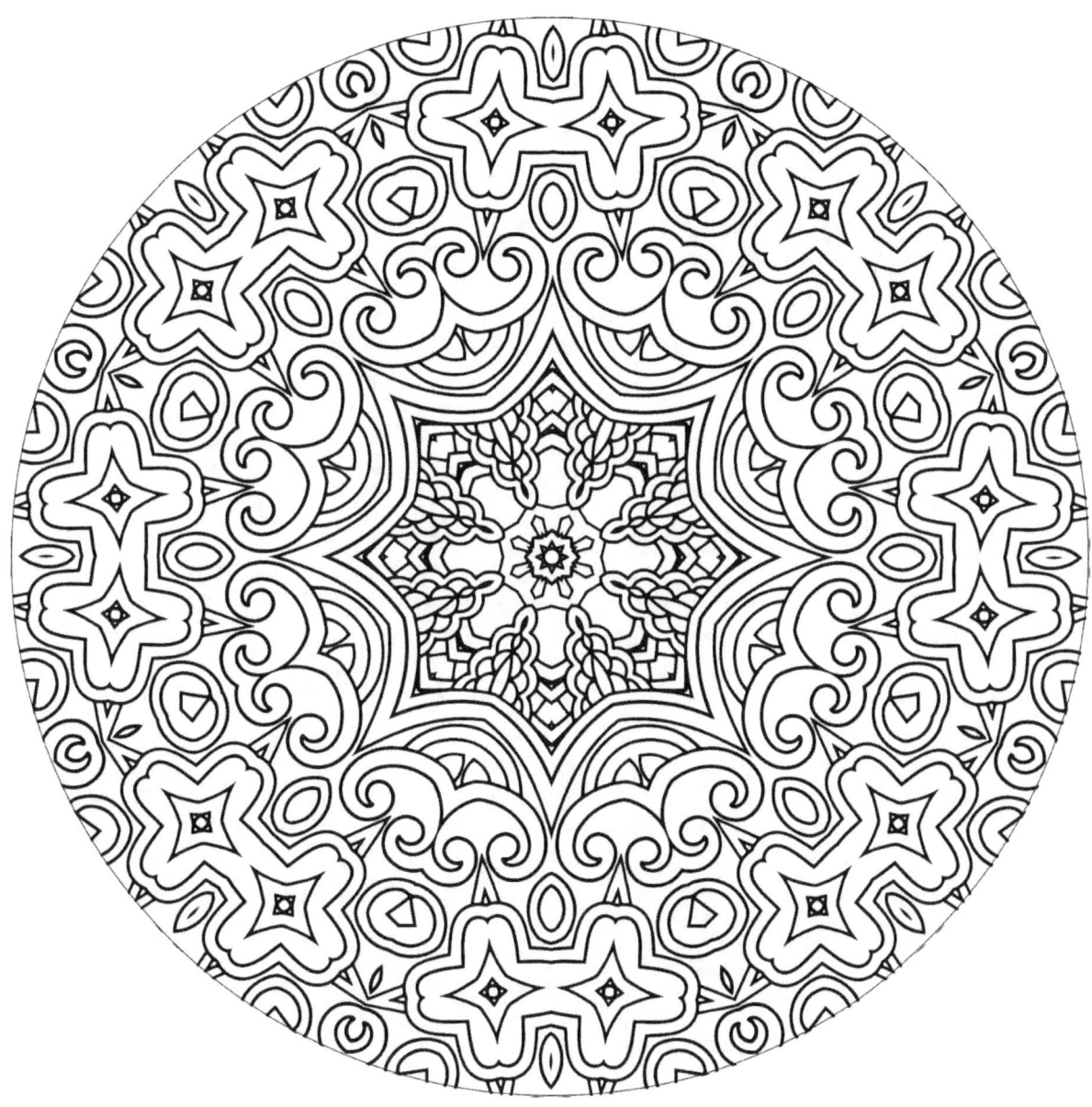

MG21

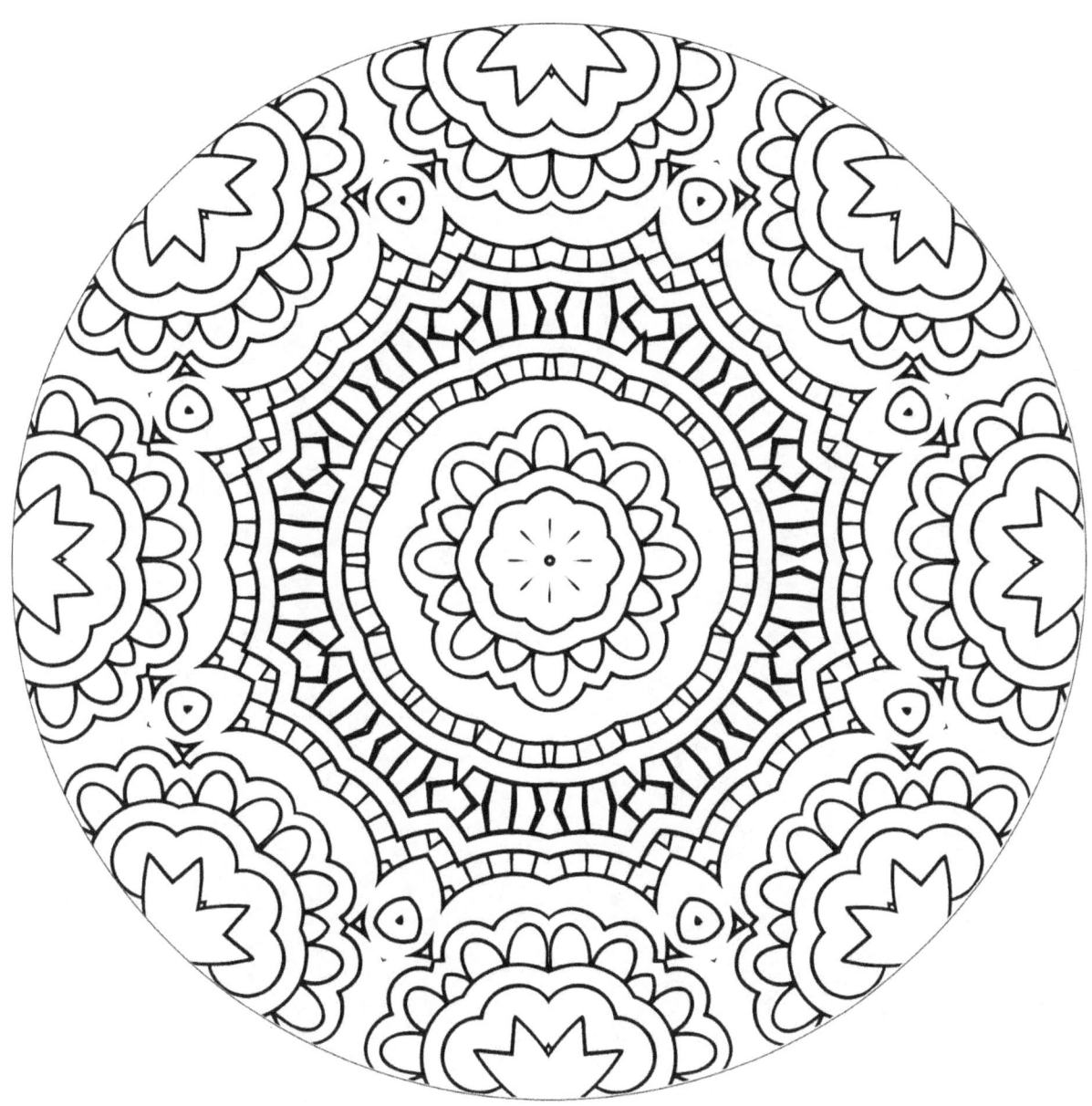

MG22

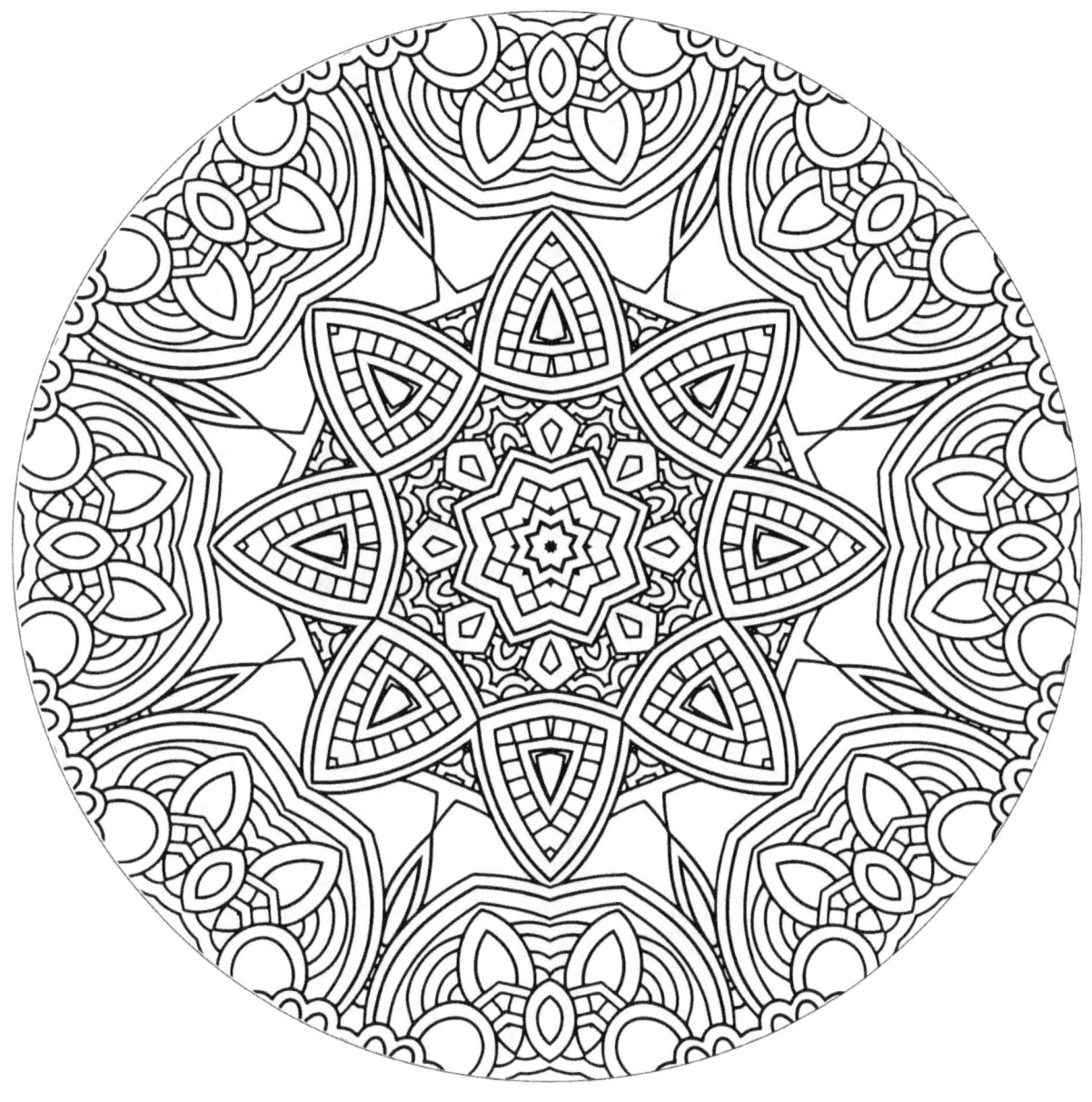

MG23

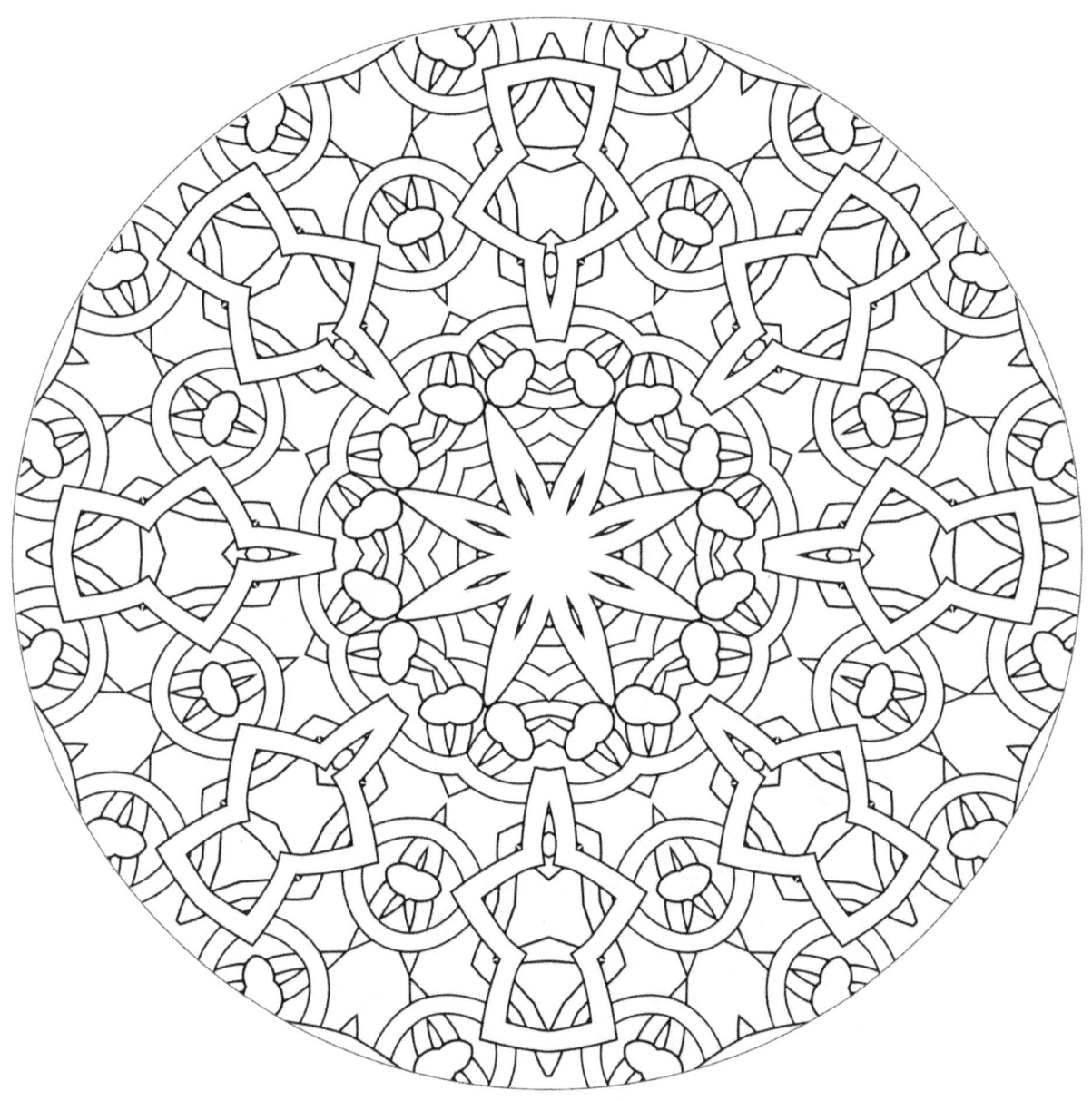

MG24

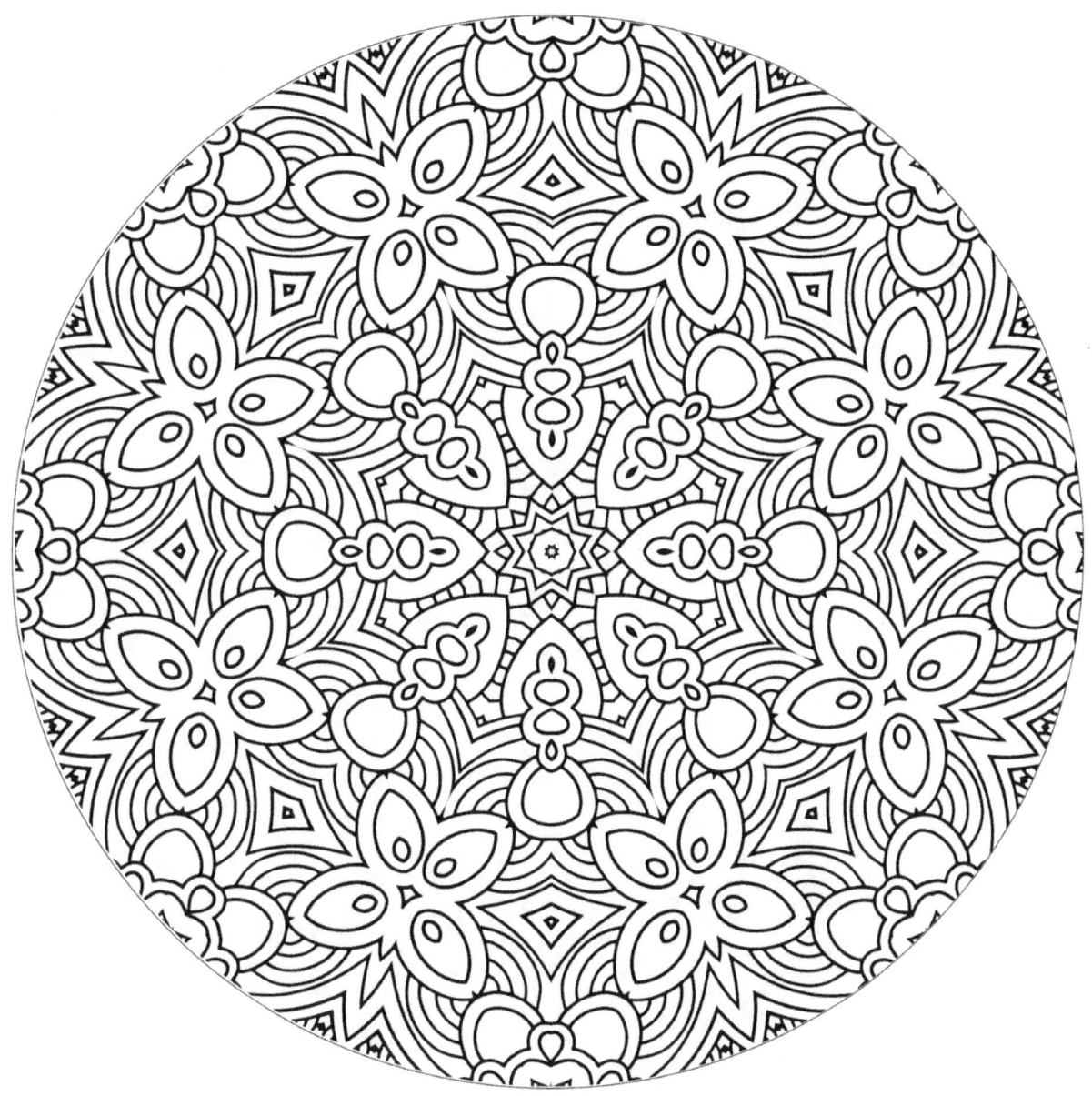

MG25

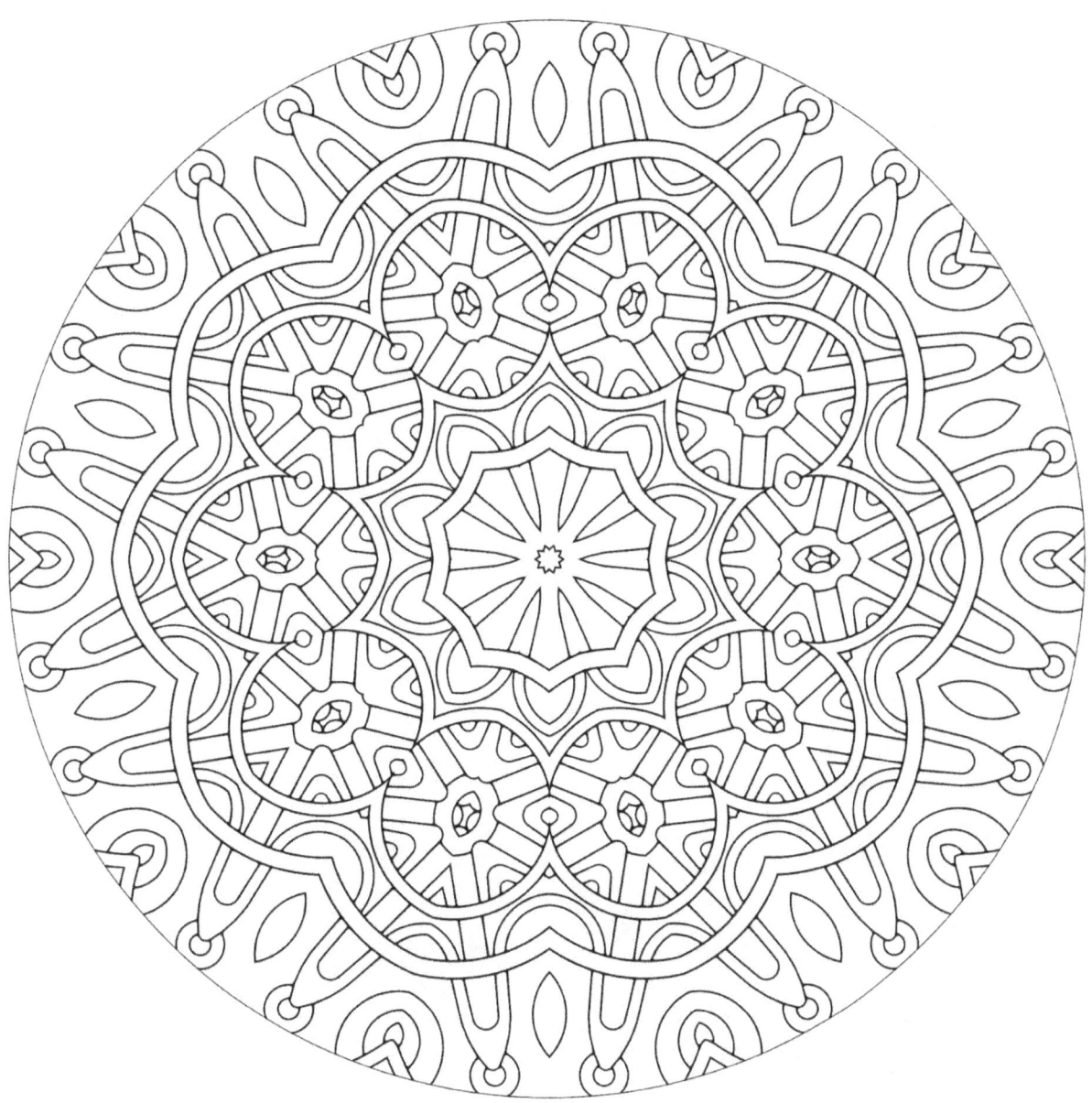

MG26

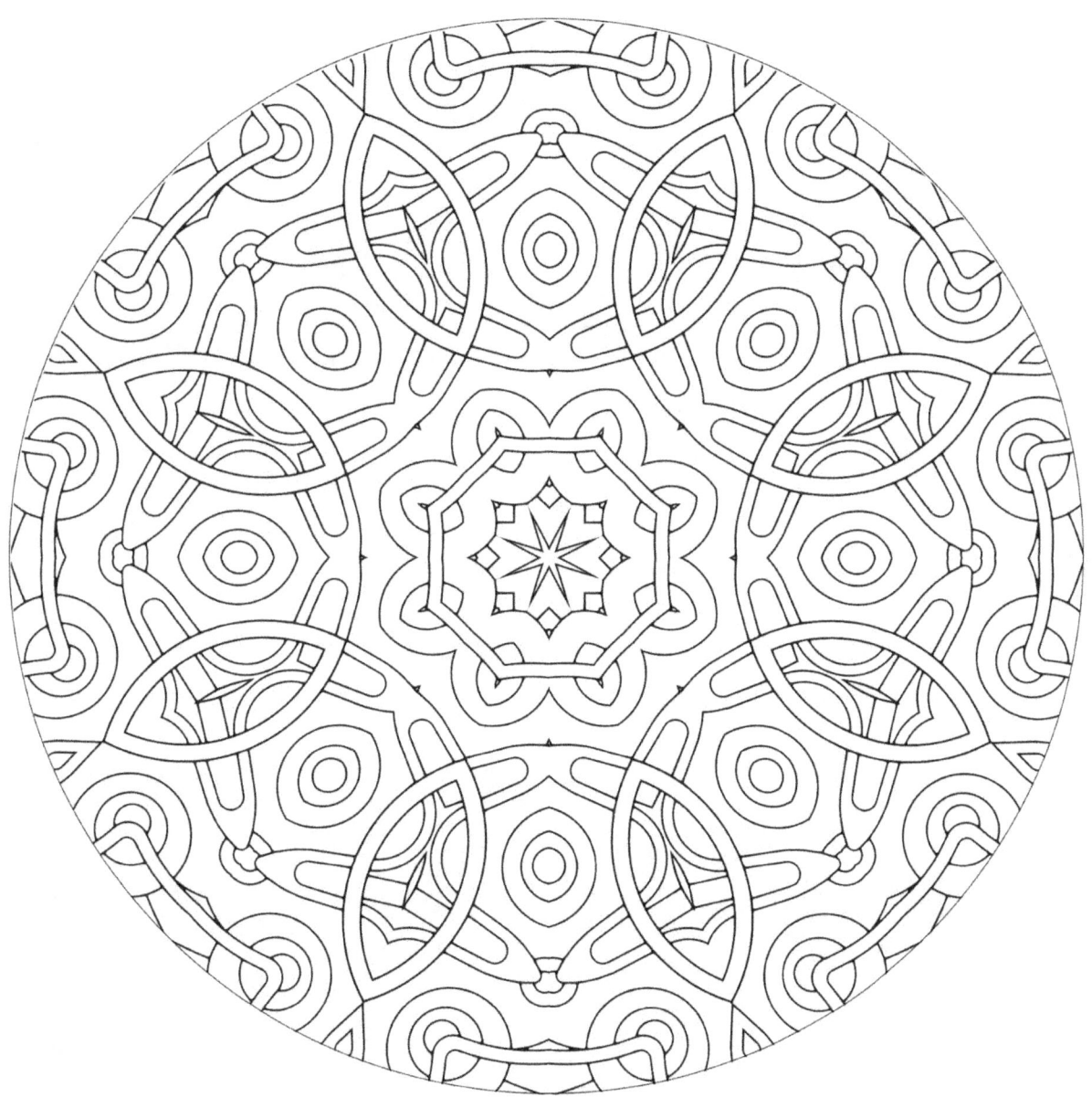

MG27

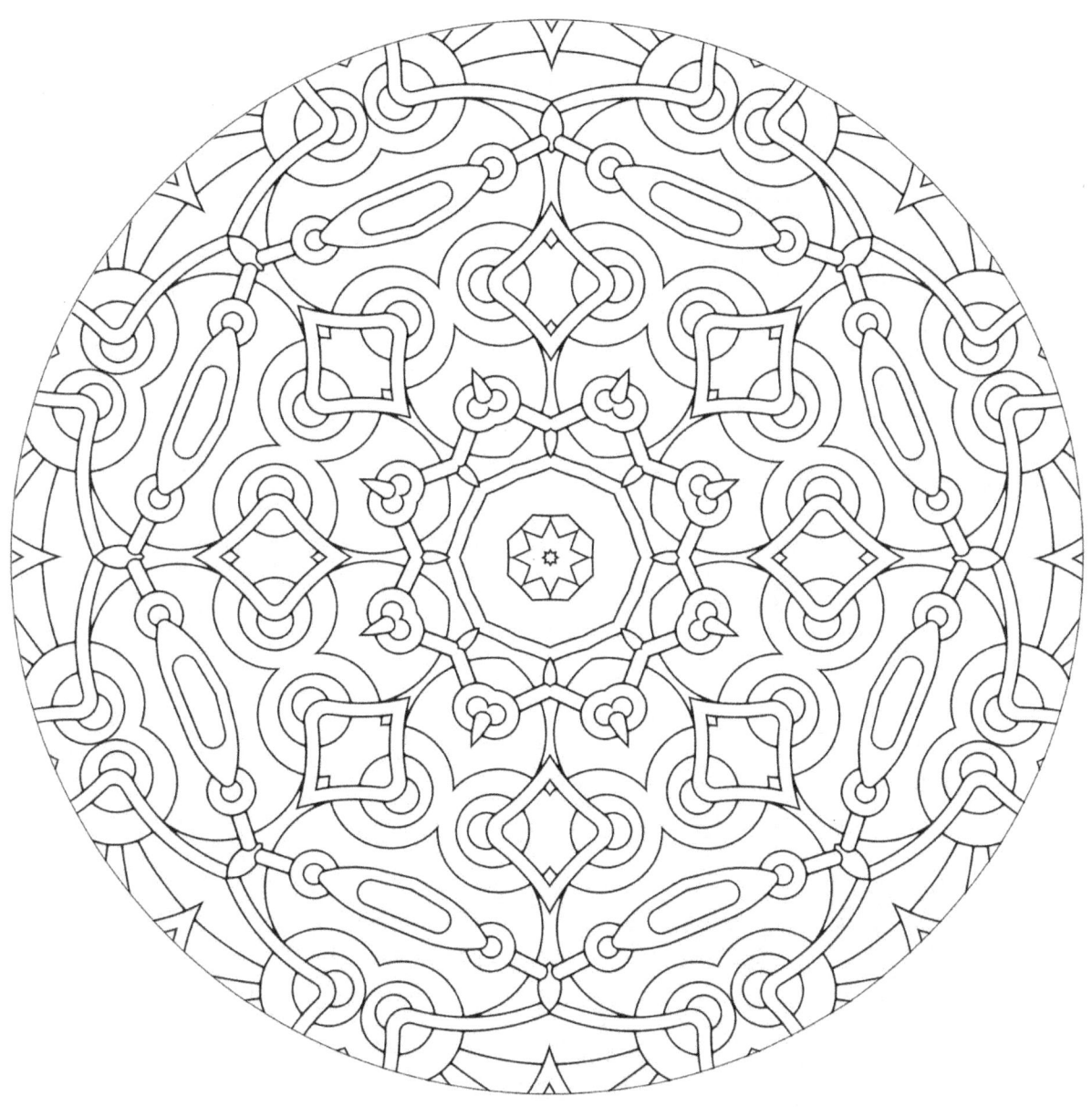

MG28

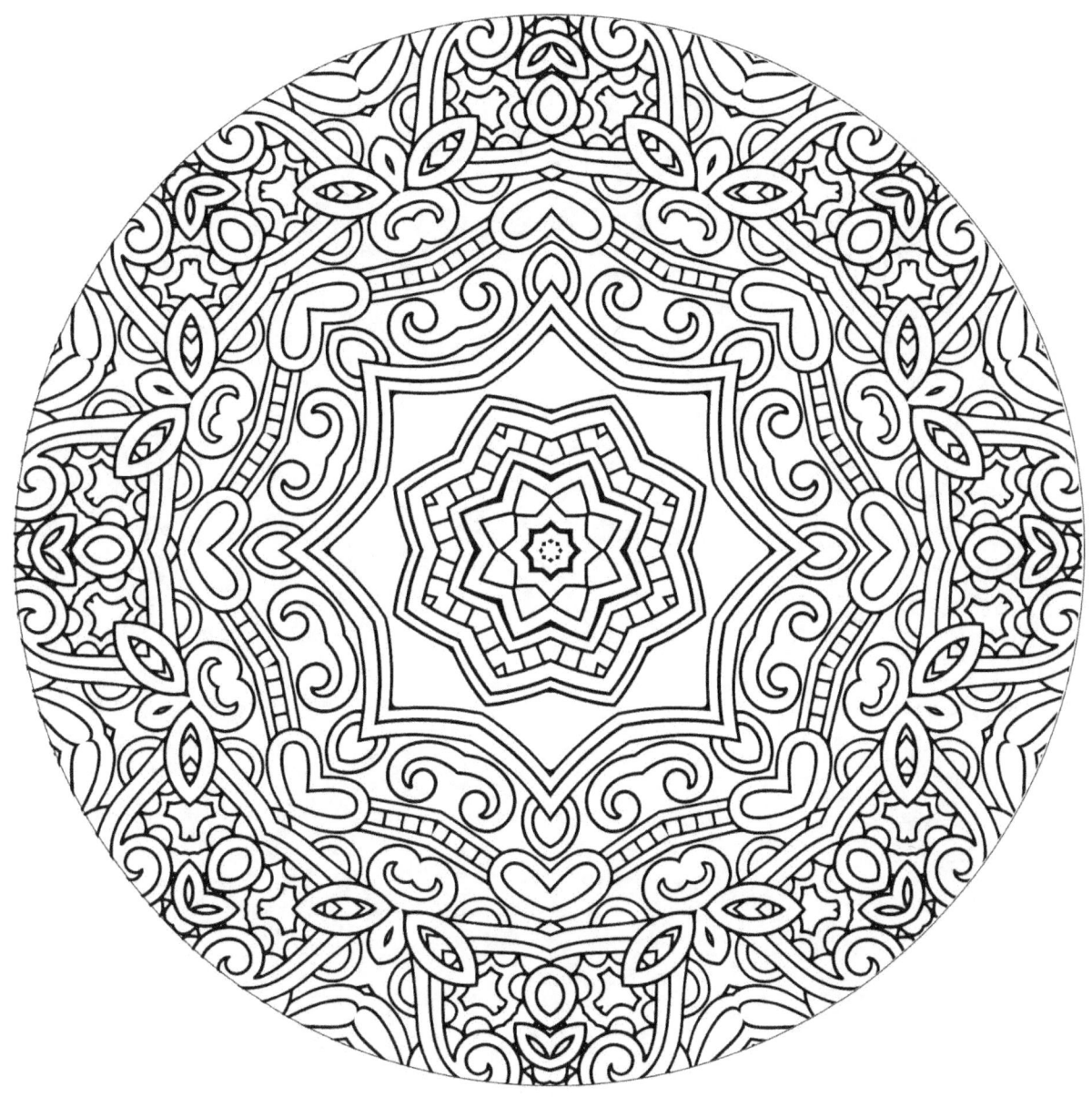

MG29

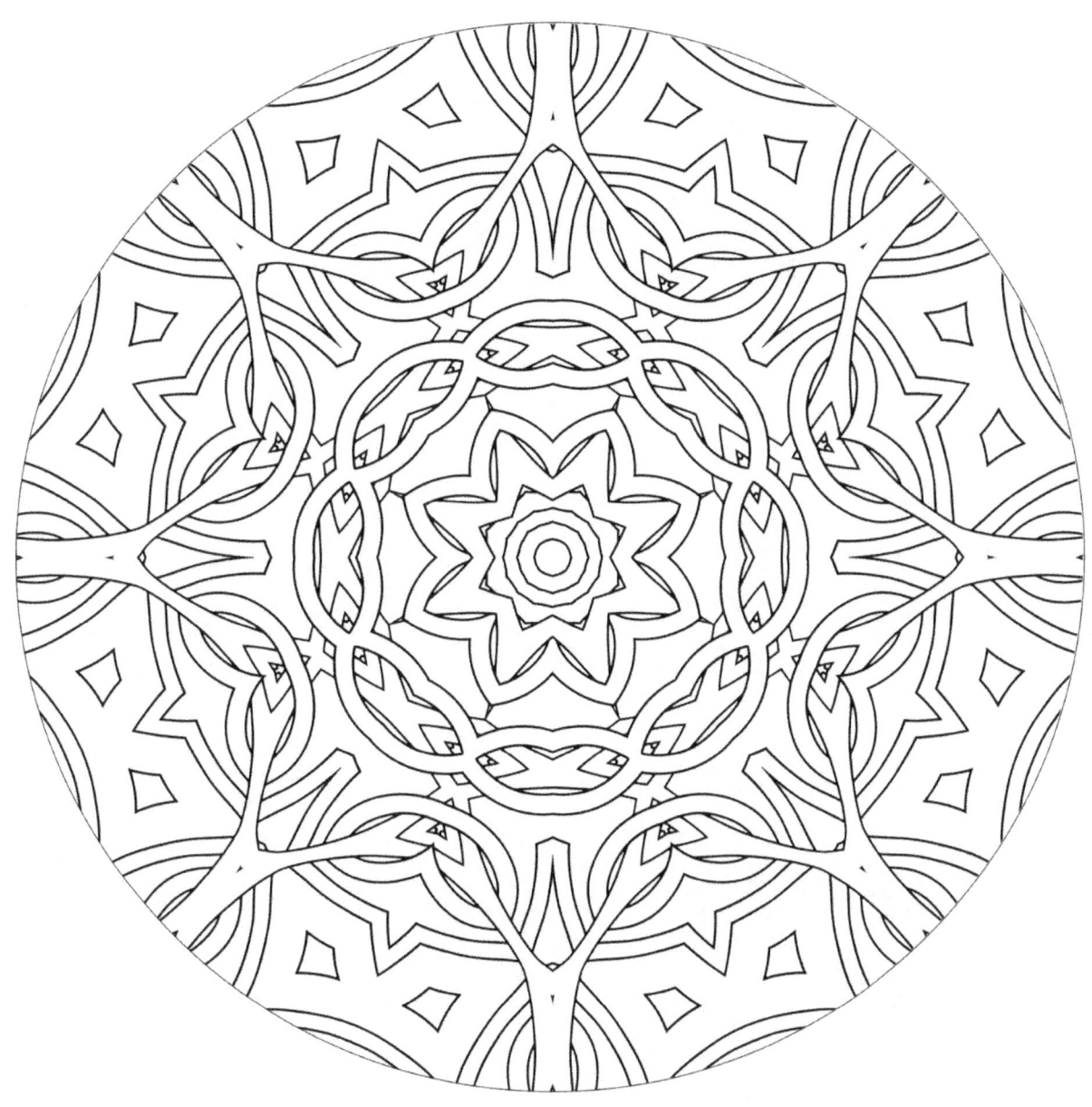

MG30

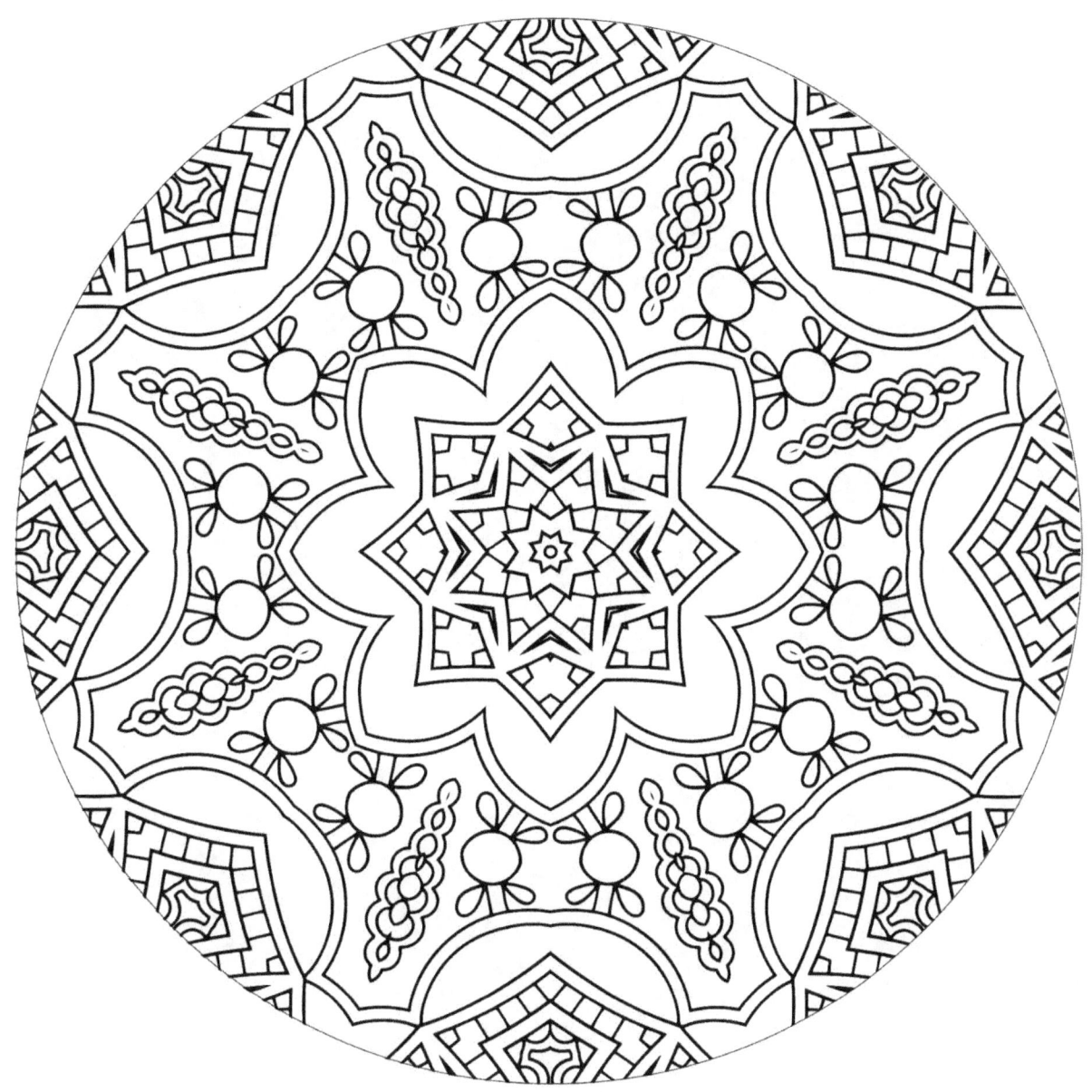

MG31

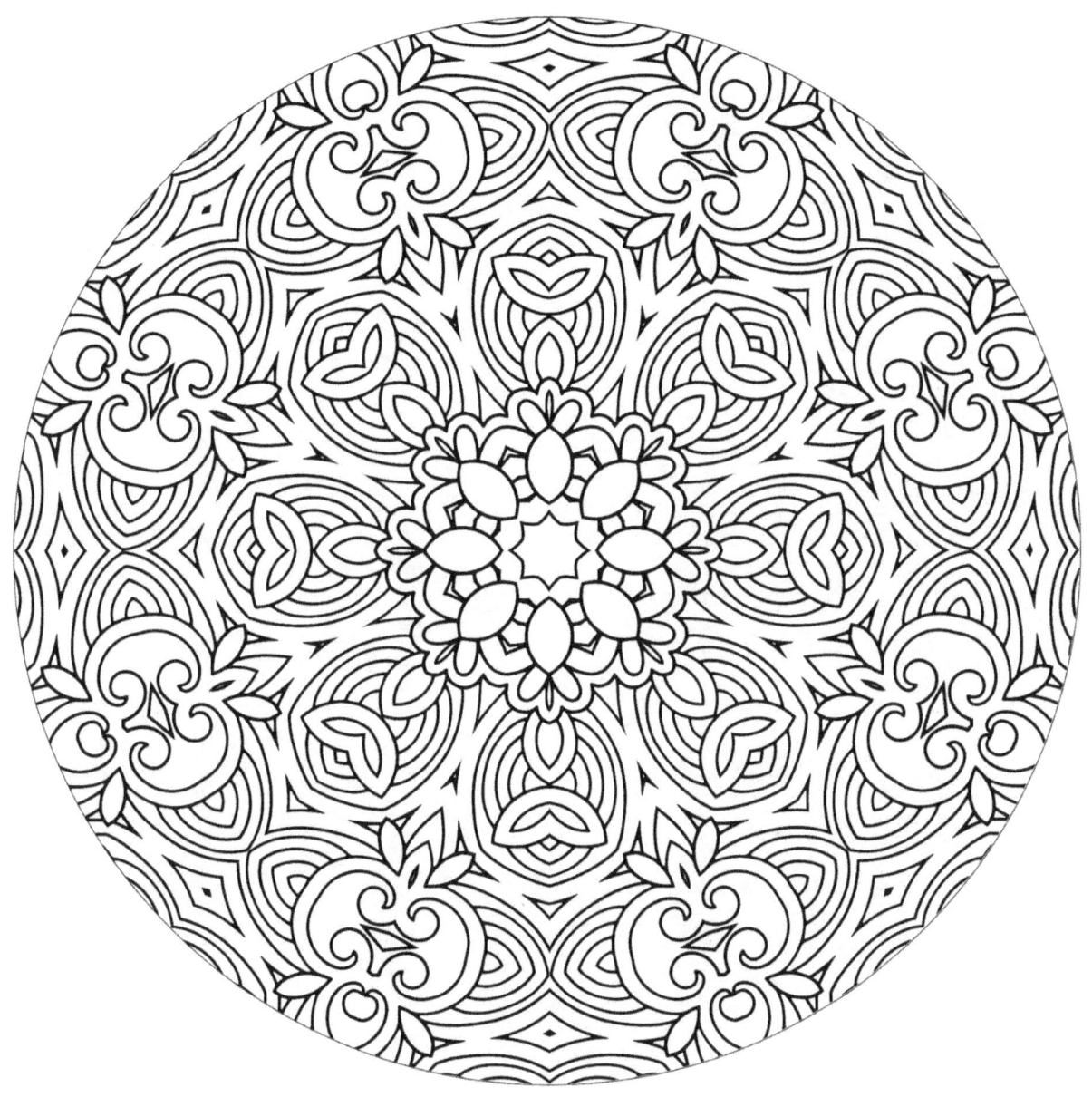

MG32

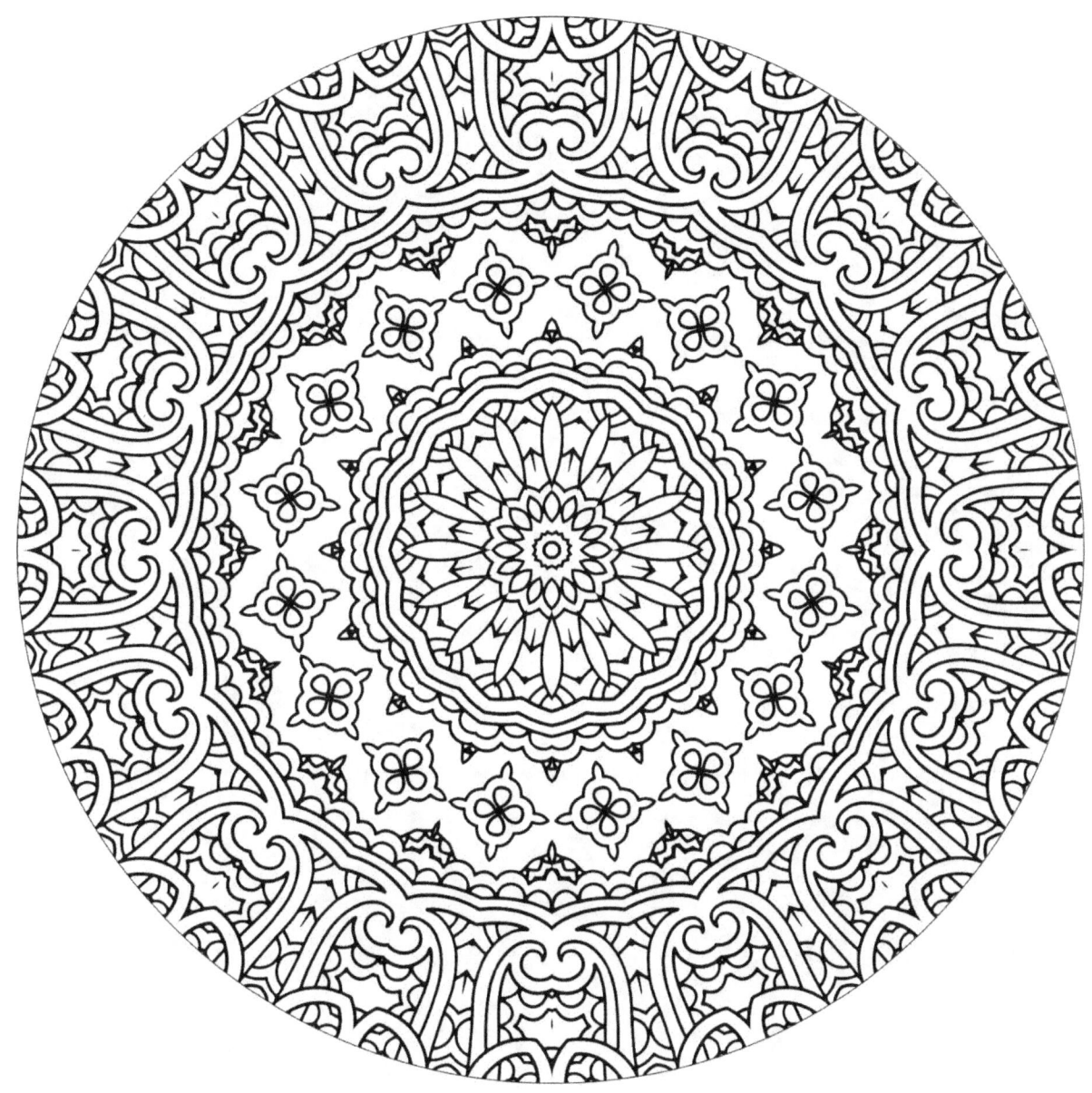

MG33

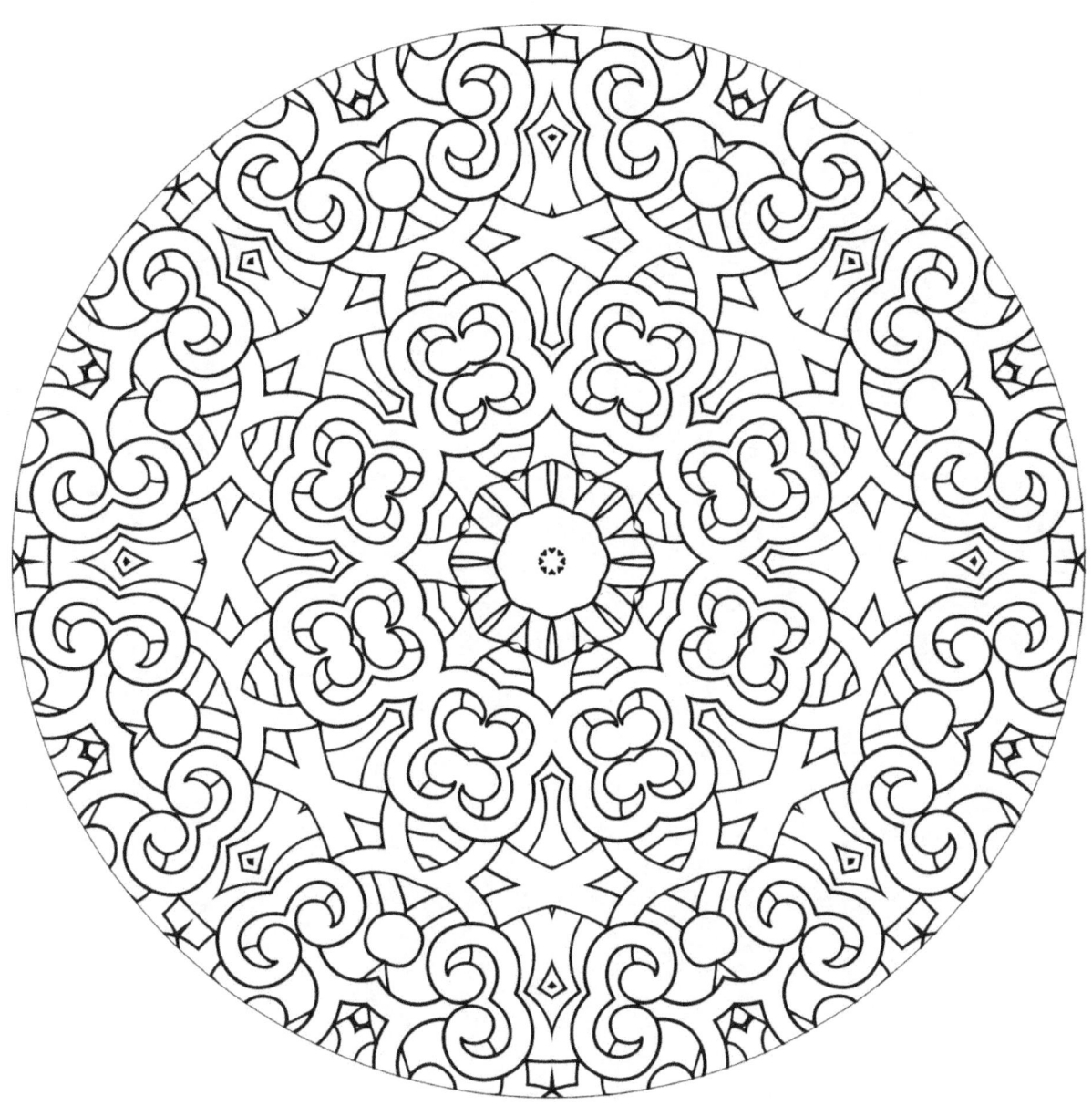

MG34

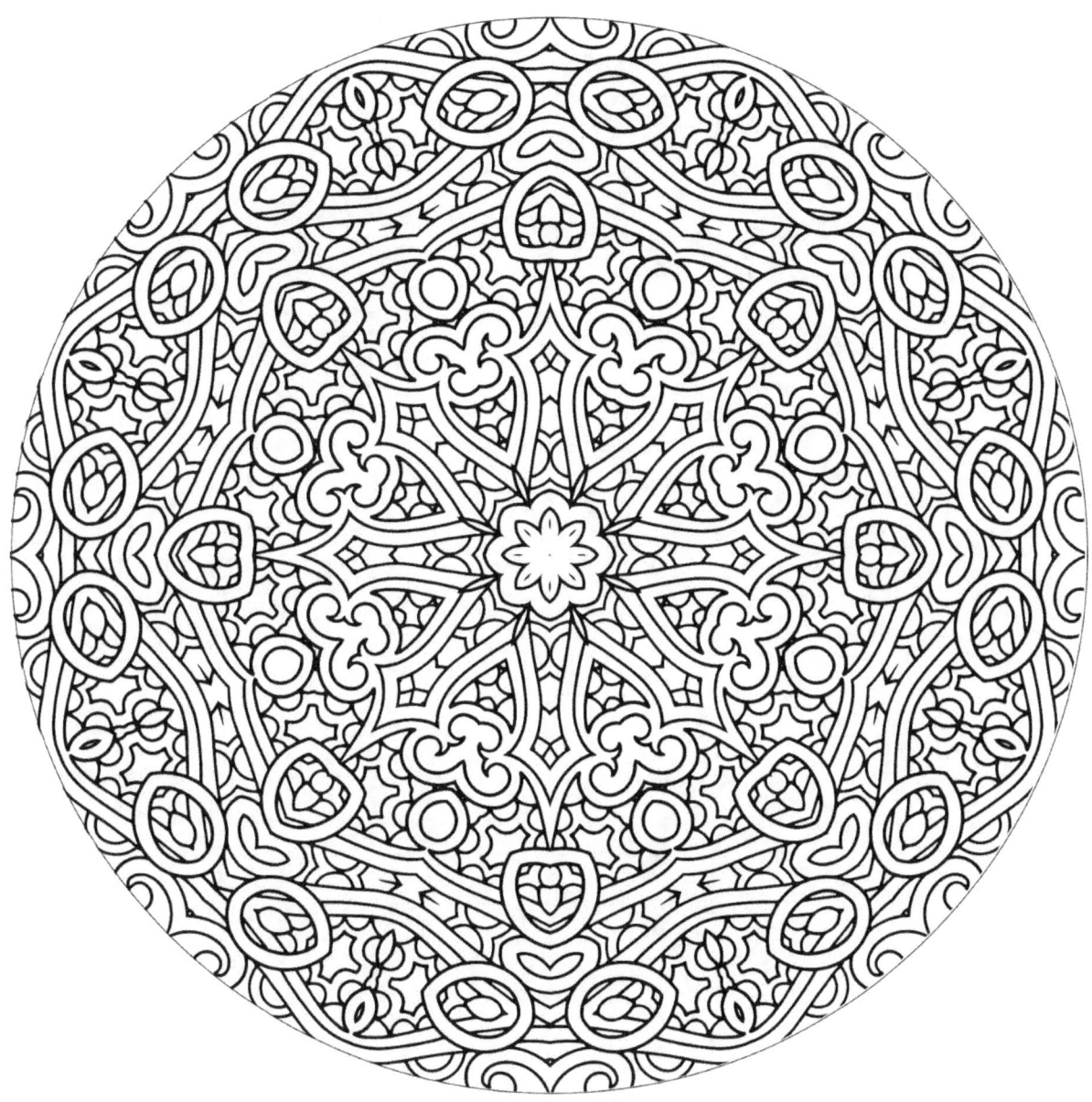

MG35

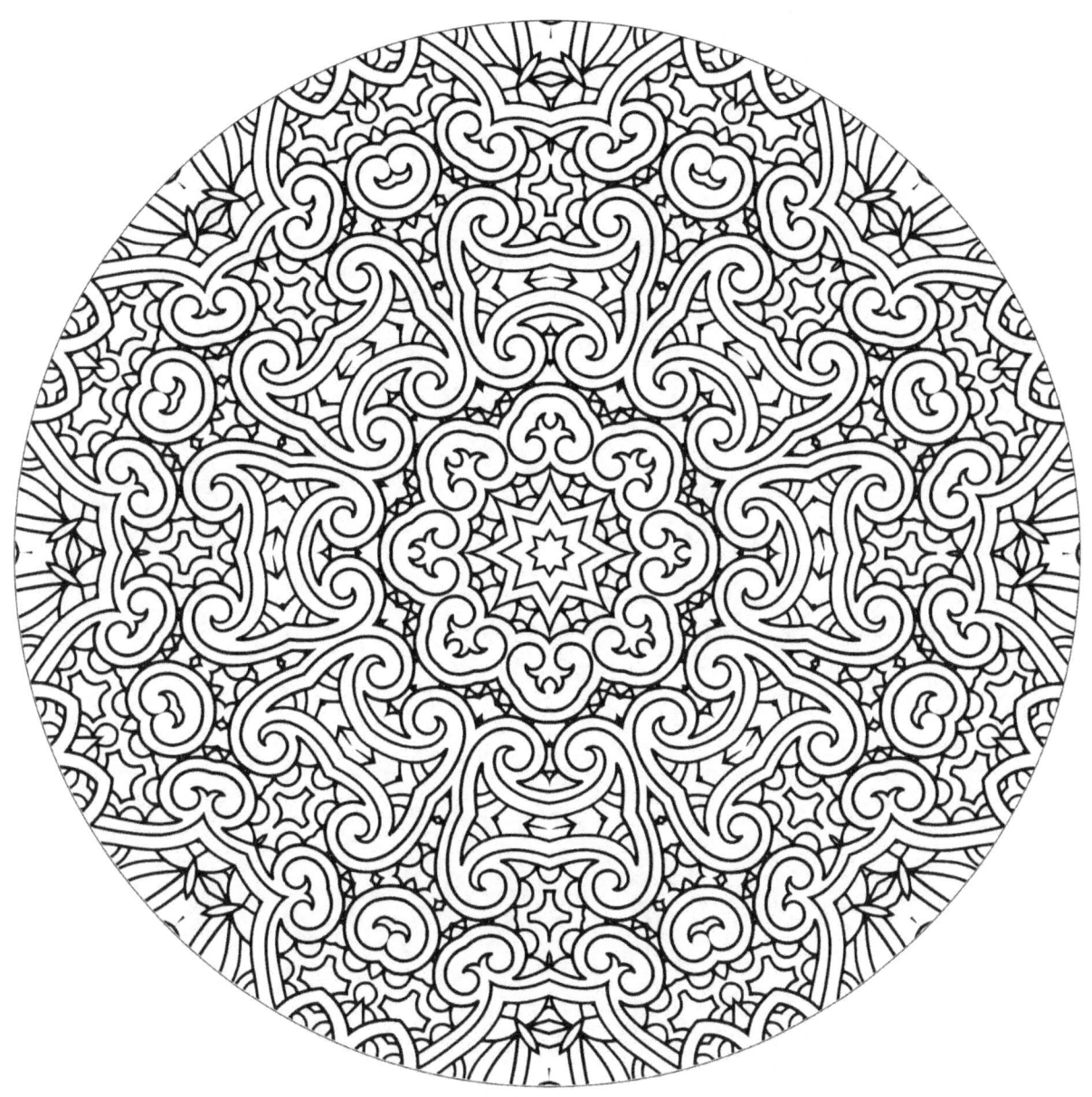

MG36

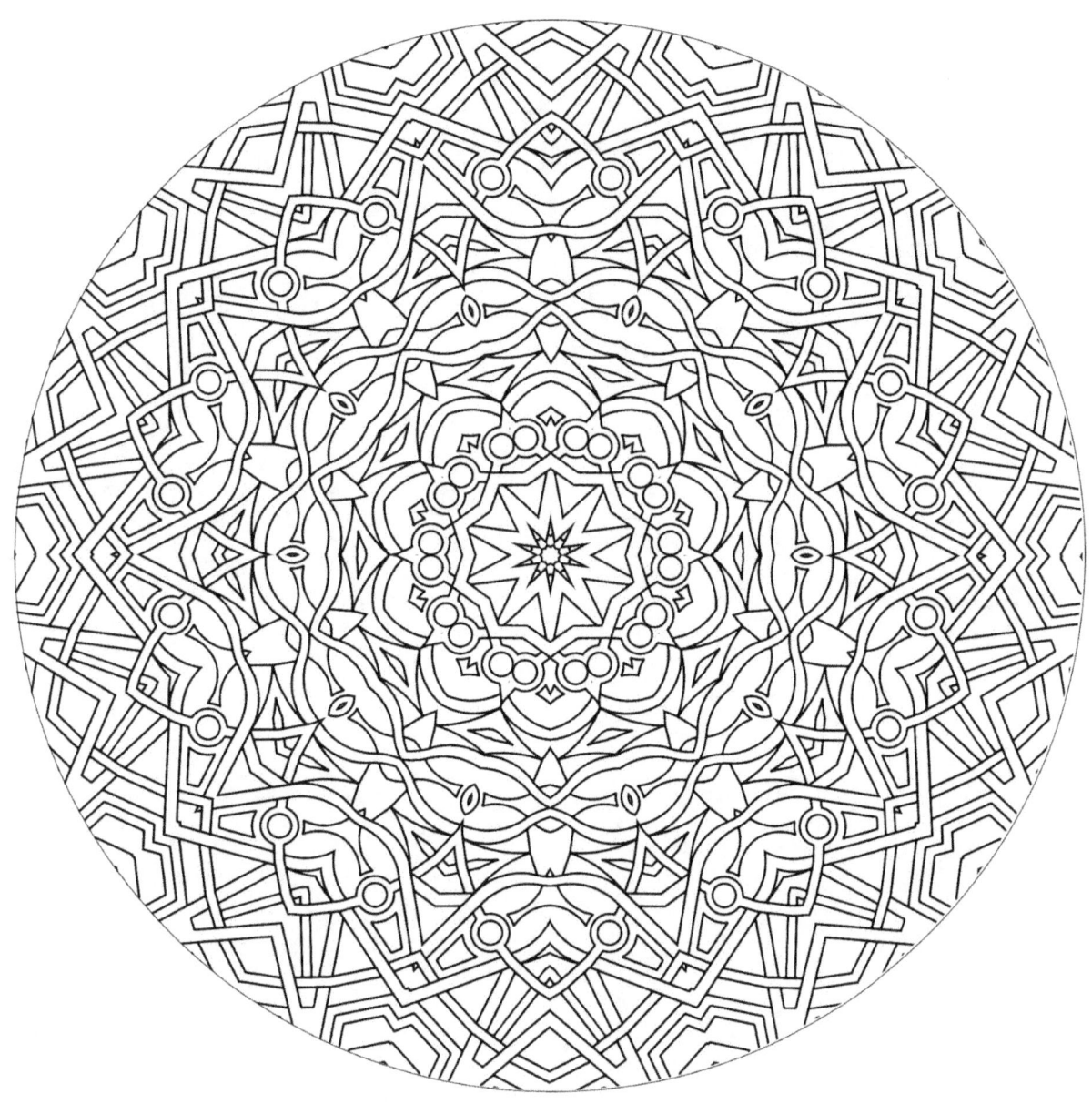

MG37

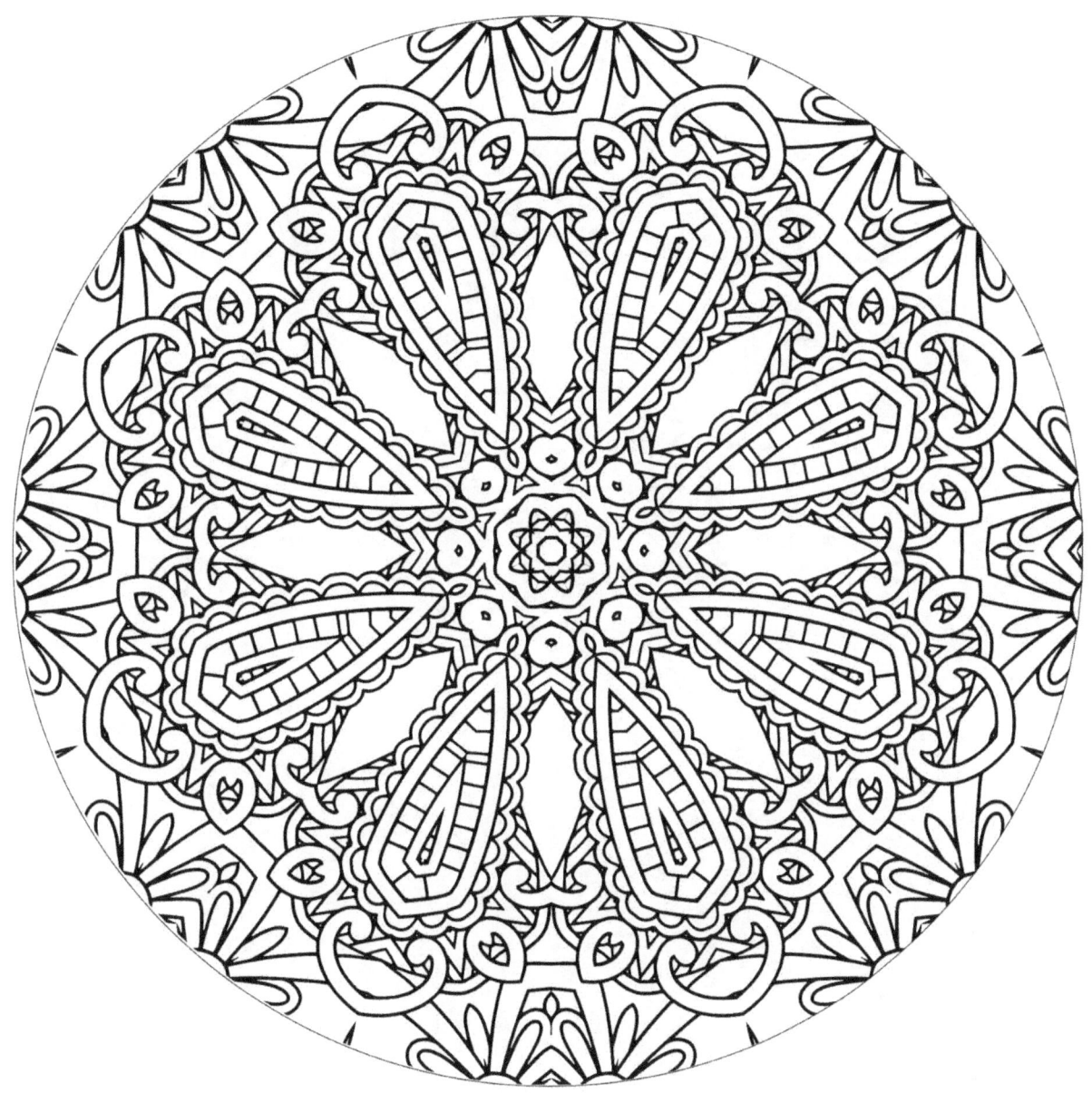

MG38

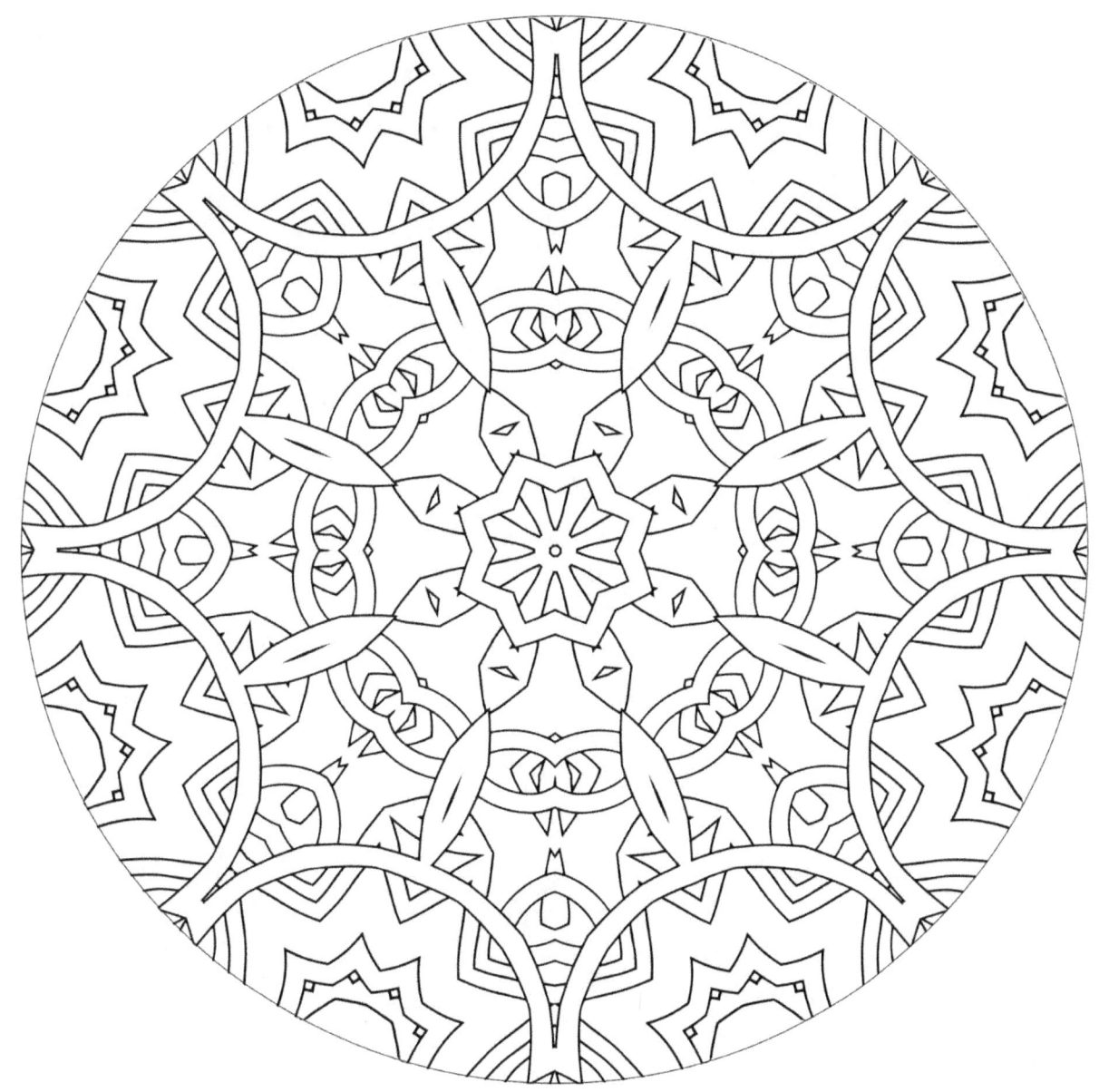

MG39

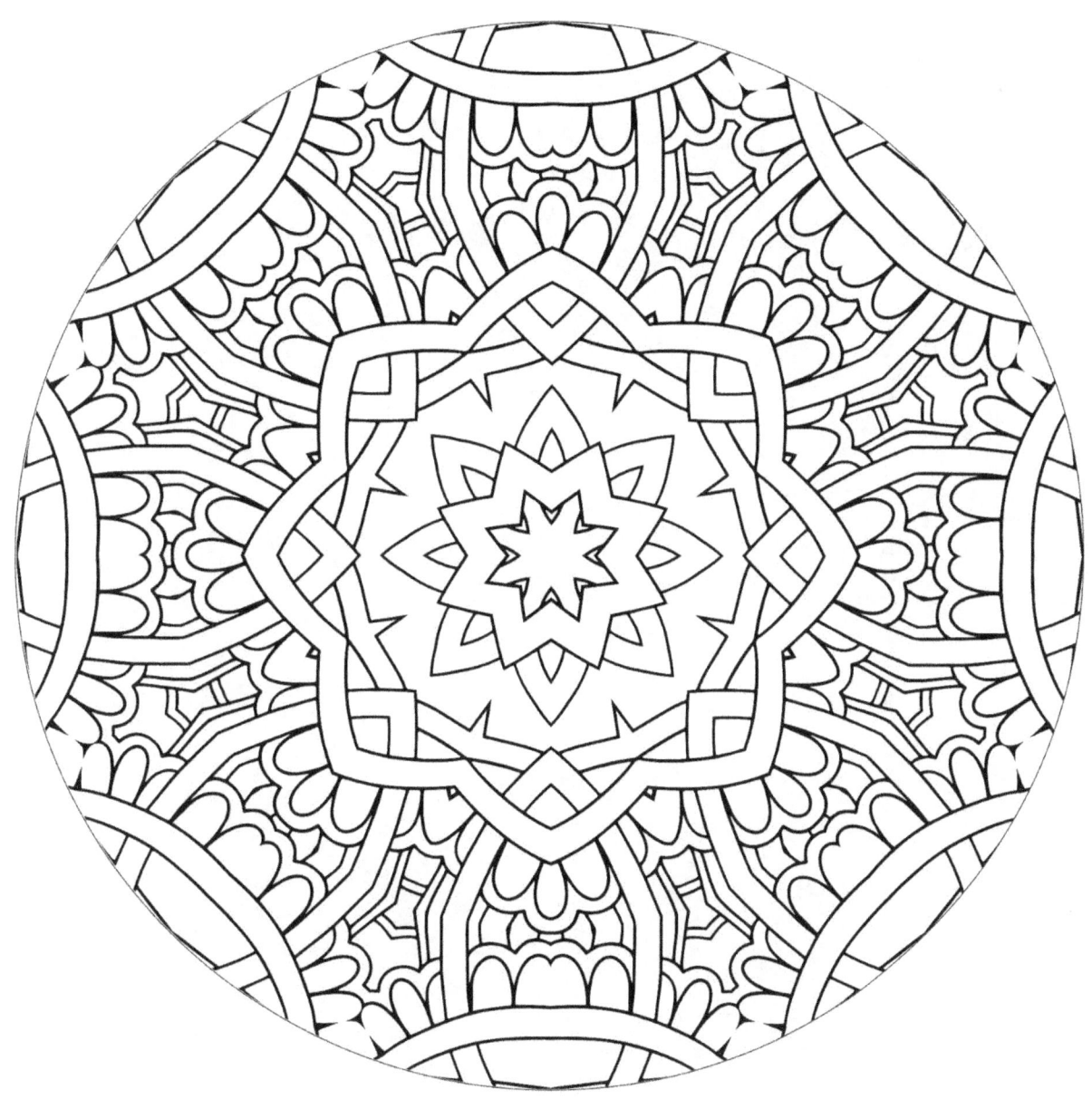

MG40

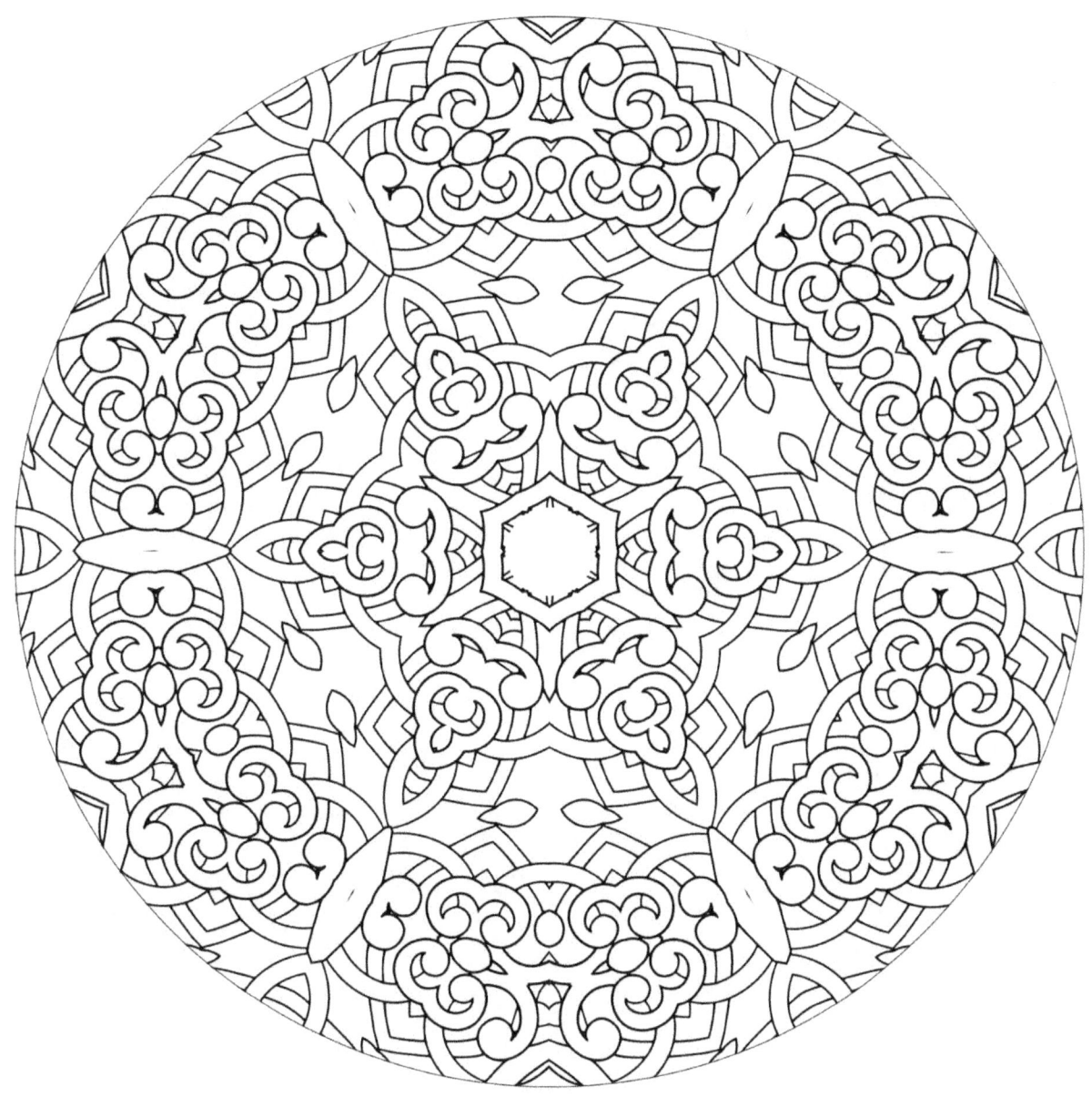

MG41

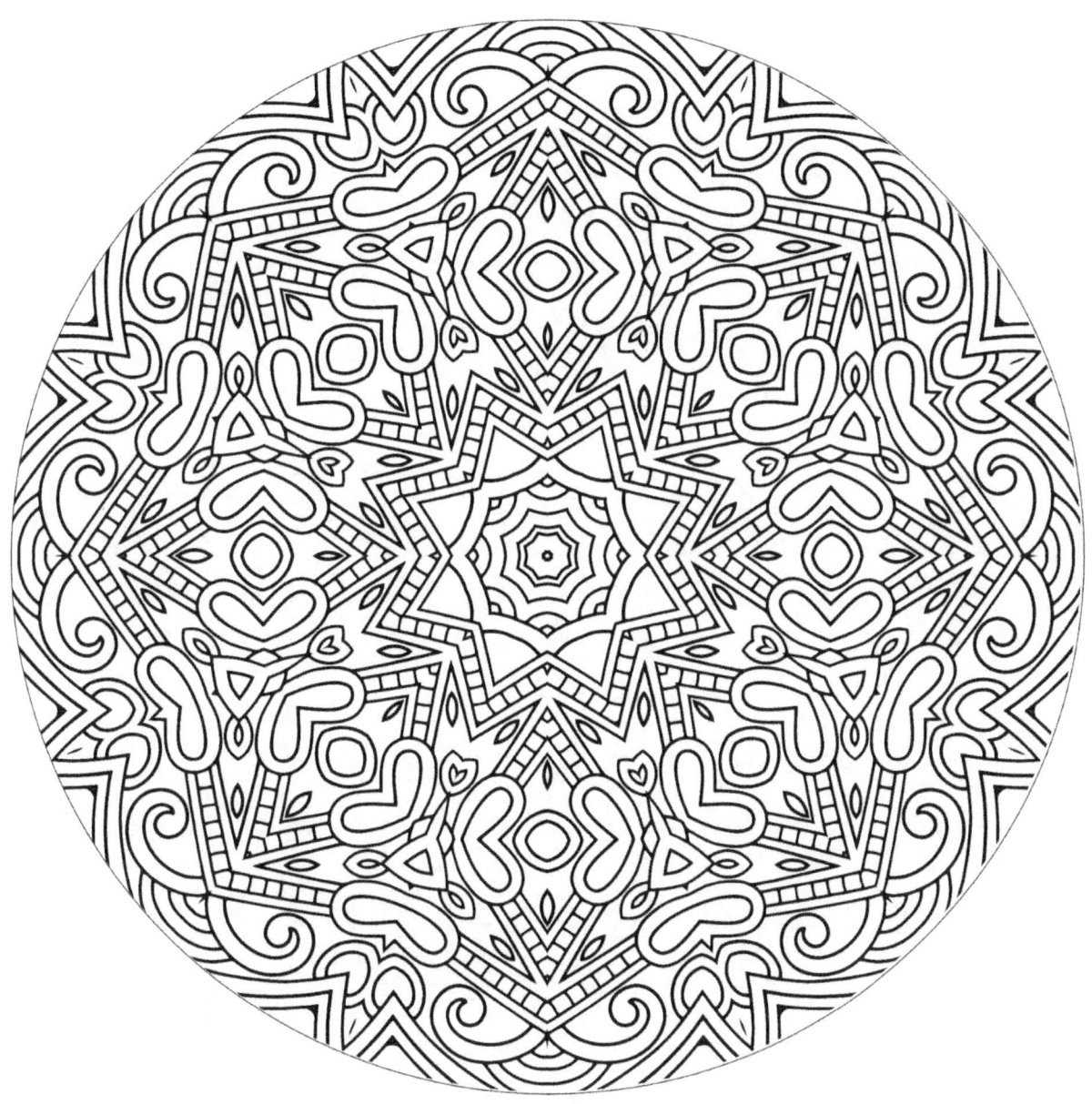

MG42

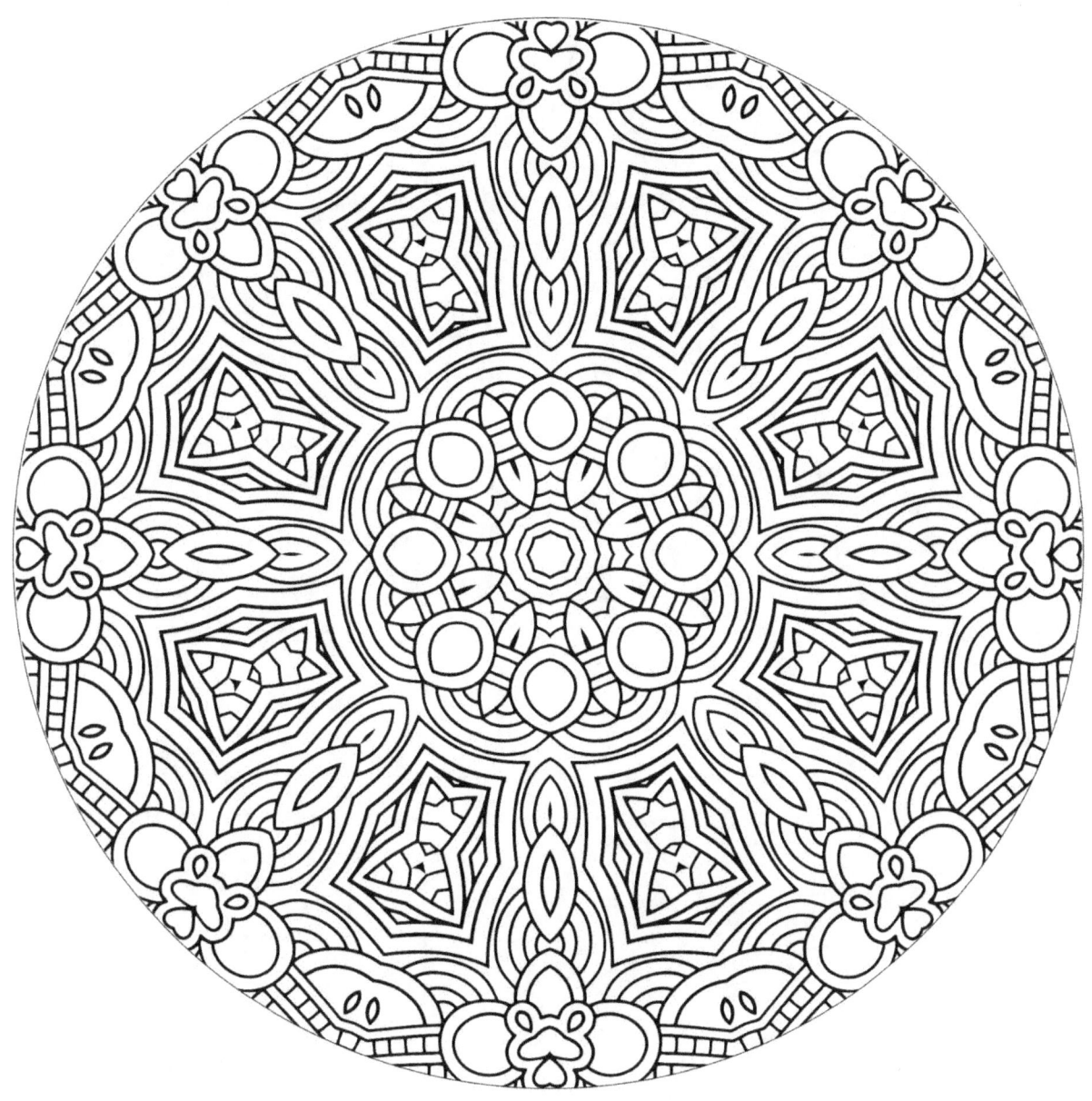

MG43

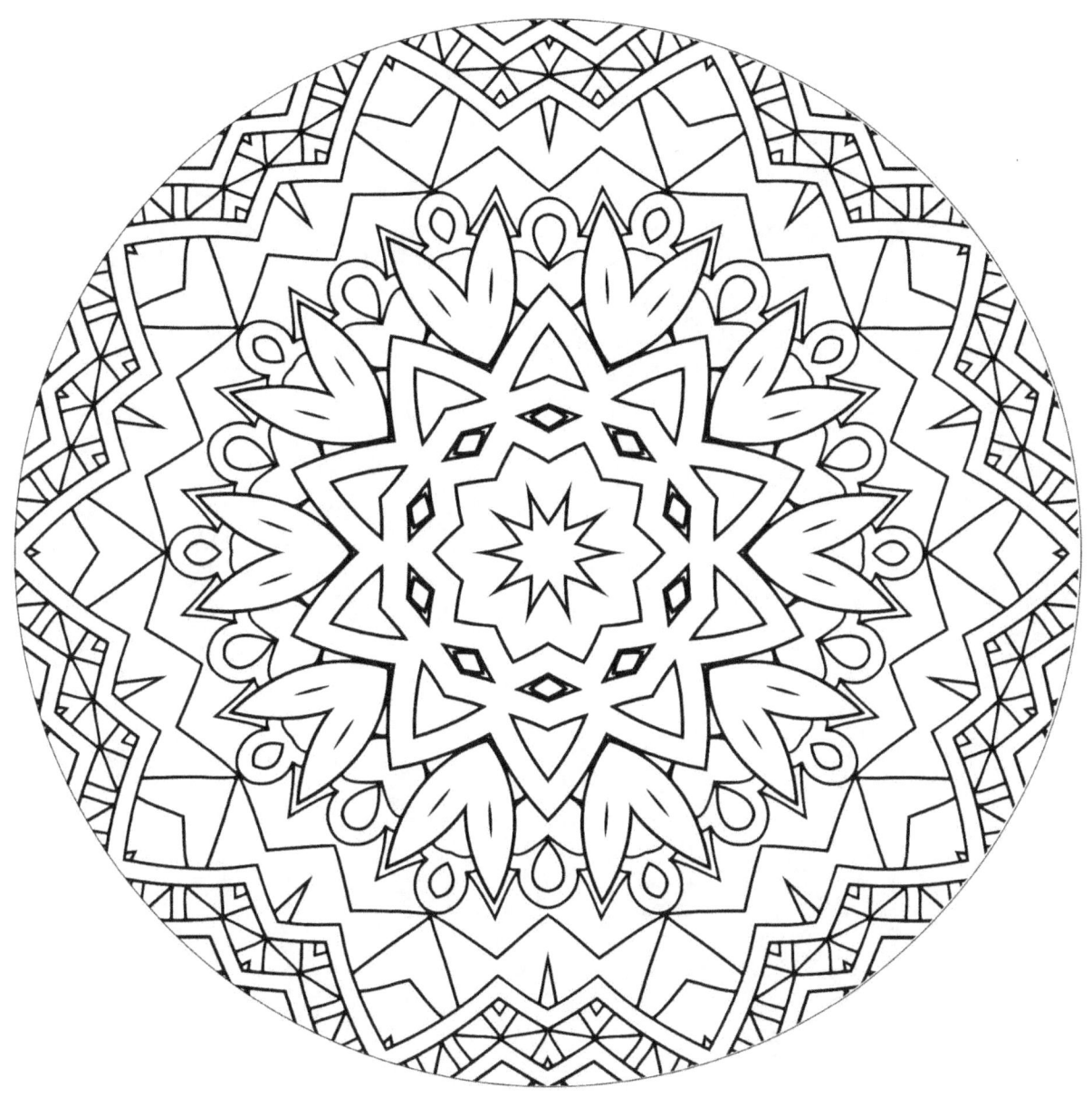

MG44

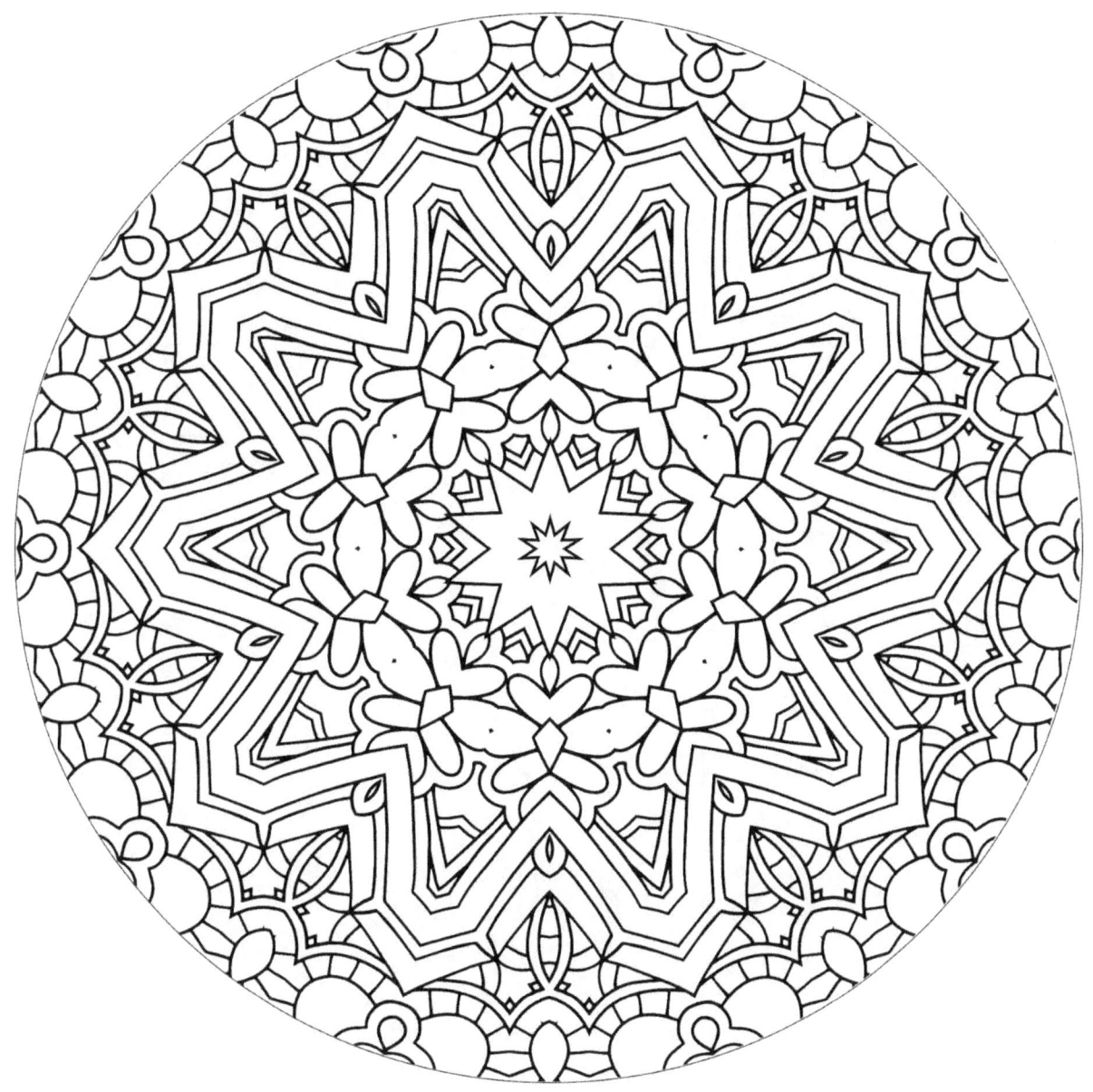

MG45

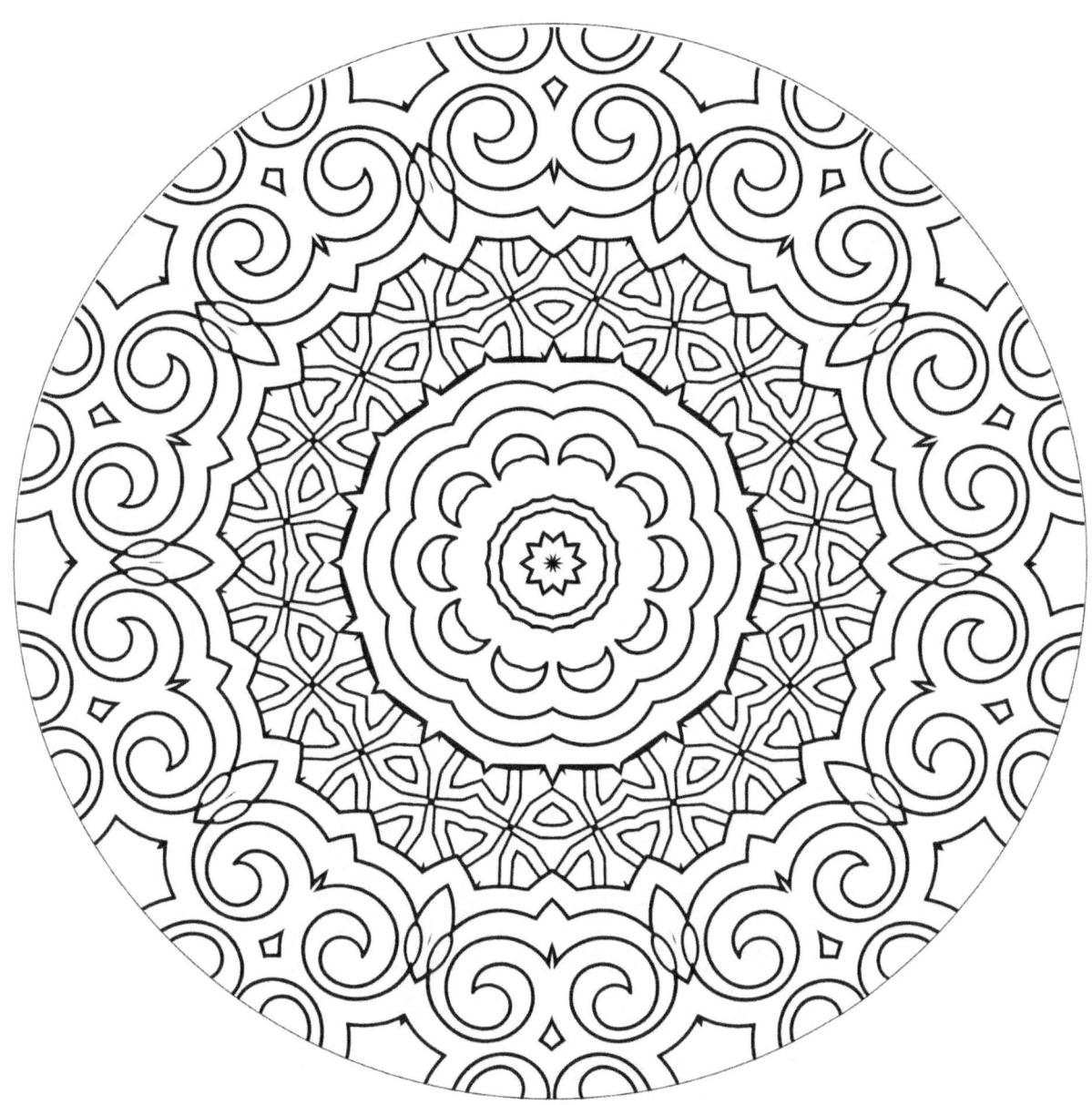

MG46

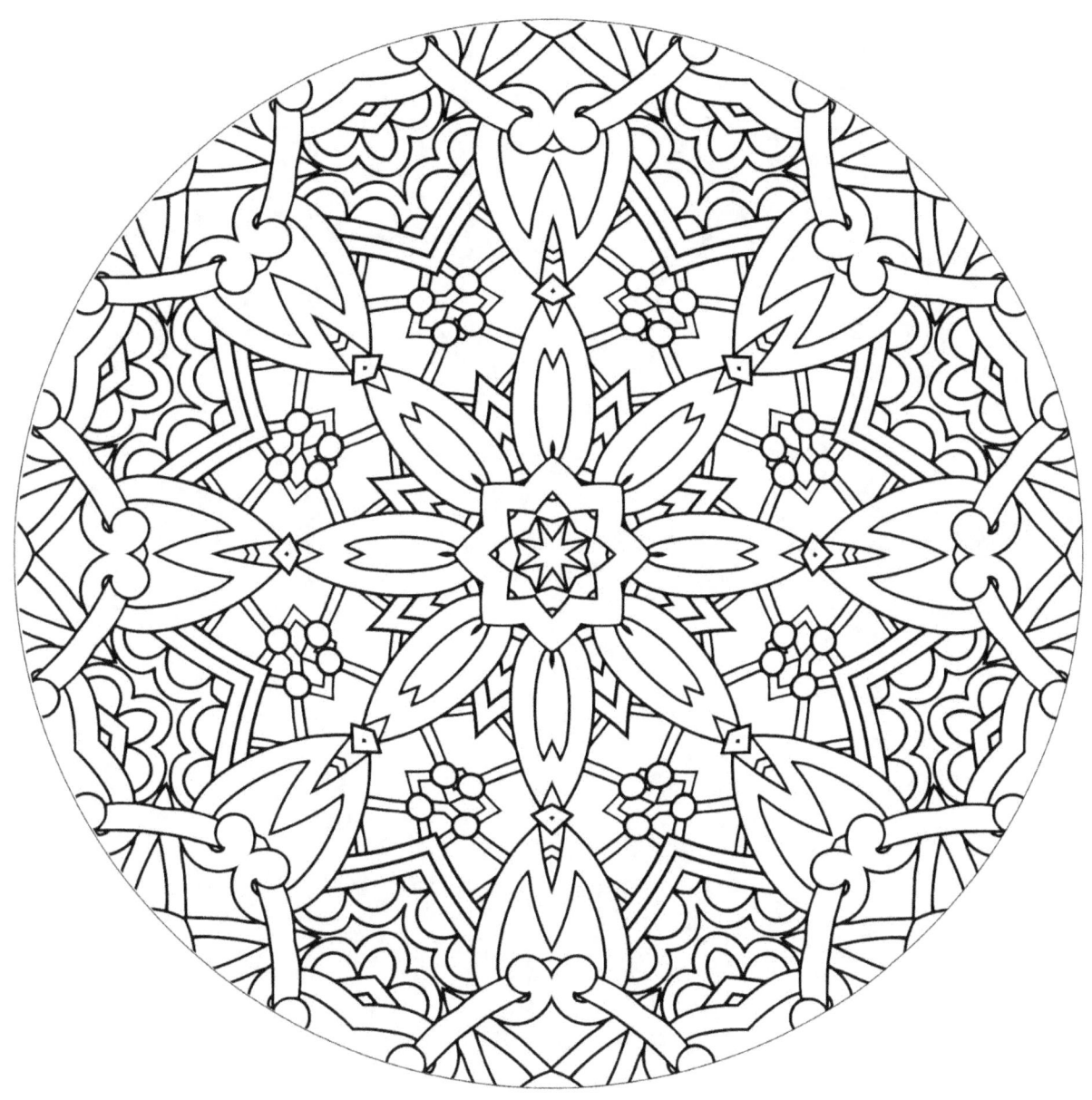

MG47

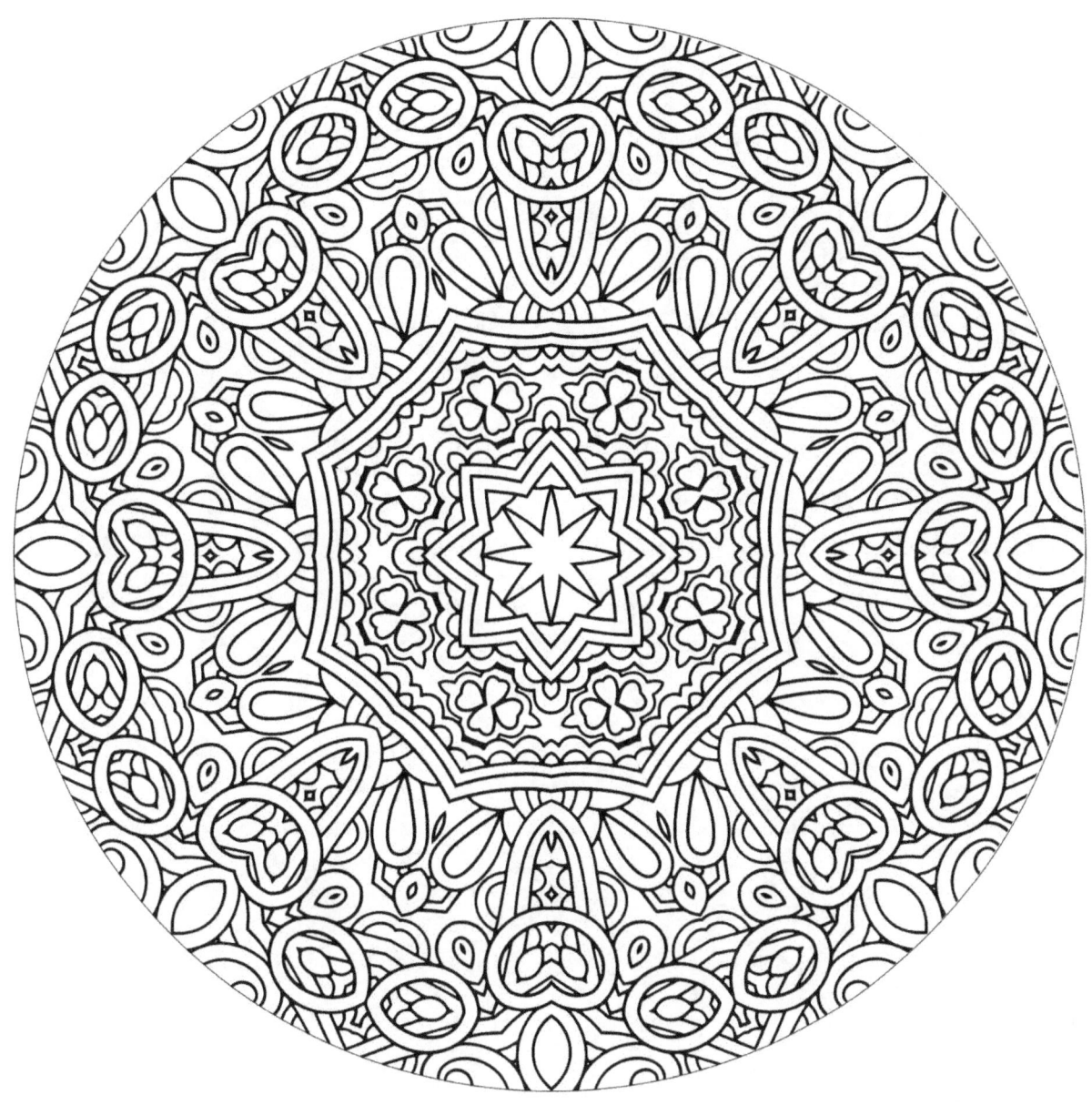

MG48

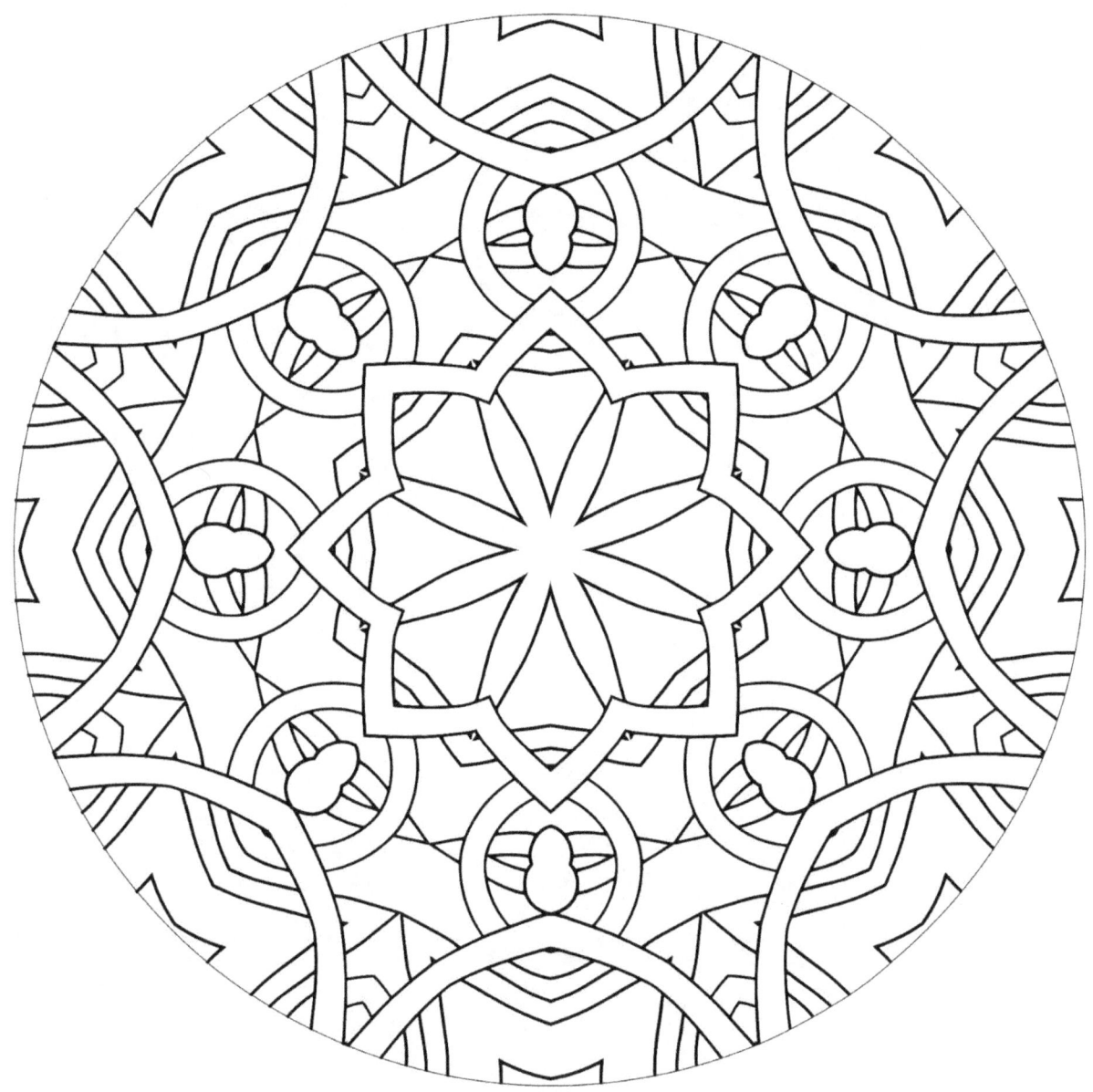

MG49

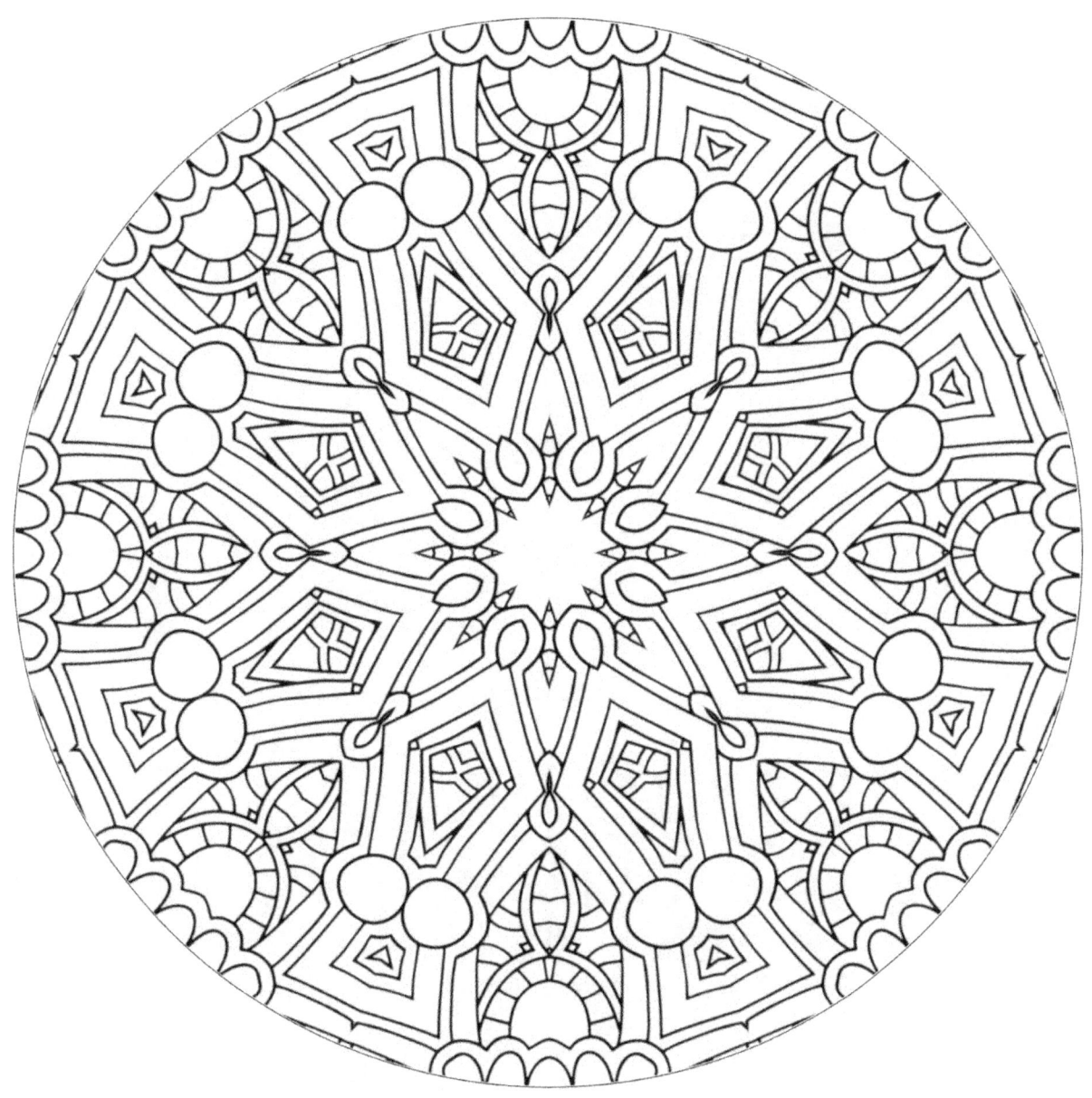

MG50

HERE IS A SECRET GIFT FOR YOU

If I could personally thank everyone that bought my book I really would, but unfortunately that is just impossible. However, I do try my best to show my appreciation with **newsletter exclusive free mandalas** and **limited time coupons** for purchases of my coloring books only for those who subscribe to my secret newsletter and follow me on this wonderful coloring journey.

So, would you do me the honor of subscribing to my newsletter? It is **completely free** and within a few days you will receive some great free downloads including **special mandalas** from my secret collection straight into your inbox! These mandalas will never be published as they are exclusive to my newsletter subscribers only. And I think you will love the mandalas!

I will also be sending you fun and useful reading on mandalas and coloring. Once in a while, I also organise super exciting coloring competitions and giveaways via my newsletter which means there is more coloring goodies to be won.

So, just click on the link below, fill out your name and email address so I know where to send you my first newsletter and get you started on this amazing coloring journey.

http://mandala.amzndownload.com

Thank you so much and see you soon!

Michelle Shea